Building Faith Brick by Brick

An Imaginative Way to Explore the Bible with Children

Emily Slichter Given

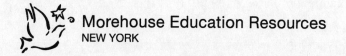

Morehouse Education Resources
NEW YORK

Morehouse Education Resources,
a division of Church Publishing Incorporated
Editorial Offices: 600 Grant Street, Suite 630, Denver, CO 80203

For catalogs and orders call:
1-800-672-1789
www.Cokesbury.com

Illustrations by Tom Lybeck.

Photos provided by the author.

ISBN-13: 978-1-60674-192-4

Emily captures the essence of the Christian story in the life of the Christian community. All of us, and children especially, are invited into an experiential, playful, and piece-by-piece exploration and building of the stories of faith. I highly recommend this book, its methods, and all the wonderful insights it brings. A must have, must use, must share book, and one that is guaranteed to bring meaning for years to come.

—The Rev. Mark Francisco Bozzuti-Jones
award winning author of *God Created* and *Jesus the Word*,
priest for pastoral care and community at Trinity Wall Street in New York City

Building Faith Brick by Brick is a fresh and practical approach to whole-community faith- formation glued together with a deep reverence for the power of stories retold and propped up with LEGO® bricks! Emily introduces us to pint-sized prophets and larger than life encounters with a wild Spirit. Her grasp of "boy faith" is brilliant—so needed right now in our churches. Warning: this guide will draw you in. You will not be the same after Emily Slichter Given is finished stirring your imagination!

—The Rev. Thomas Brackett
Missioner, New Church Starts & Missional Initiatives,
Episcopal Church Center, New York, NY

The great need in the church today is for resources, centered in Scripture, that deeply engage each child in their growing life in Christ. *Building Faith Brick by Brick* is an amazing response to the need and is so impressive because it uses a new language, a LEGO® language, for faith expression. Teachers can now teach children in Sunday school by binding religion and play by entering into a place of Joy and wonder doing theological reflection that builds upon questions of faith, brick by brick. Children can build on their own or in small groups. Everything is awesome because basic blueprints are included with a FAQ section that is absolutely so helpful to any parent or educator. This curriculum can serve as a powerful tool to aid congregations and Christian families as they pursue their goal to pass the faith to the next generation.

—The Rev. Robyn Szoke-Coolidge
Dean, Stevenson School for Ministry, Diocese of Central PA

Like some of the more interesting inventions that have shown up serendipitously or because of pressing necessity, *Brick by Brick* is a program that we've needed for a while and didn't know we needed. The individual lessons are fun, full of good, tasty content and blooming like the yeast of Jesus' parables with provocative "wondering" questions. I really appreciated, however, two things that we rarely see elsewhere: Emily's research into what she calls "boy faith" and her advice on doing Bible with kiddos, both in the introductory section and well worth reading. *Building Faith Brick by Brick* belongs on the bookshelves of our congregations; more than that, it belongs in the hands and in the playbooks of everyone responsible for the Christian Formation of children.

—Victoria L Garvey,
Associate for Lifelong Christian Formation,
Episcopal Diocese of Chicago, Chicago, Illinois

Building Faith Brick by Brick is a dynamic and palpable approach for children to encounter stories of faith in a rich new way. This acclaimed hands-on method of Christian Formation invites children's imaginations to take flight, and when this happens, the stories soon become real...block by block.

—Roger Hutchison
Canon for Children's Ministries at Trinity Episcopal Cathedral in Columbia, SC
and author of *The Painting Table; A Journal of Loss and Joy*

In *Building Faith Brick by Brick*, Emily Given provides a creative, clear, and comprehensive resource for scripture studies with children and LEGO® bricks. Whether you find a place for these wonderfully fun and surprisingly deep activities in Sunday School, Vacation Bible School, Children's Chapel, in school or at home, this is a book that will fully engage both kids and the adults who teach them. It's also an invitation to explore the Bible unlike anything else on your bookshelf. You'll want this book, and chances are, you'll want lots of LEGO® bricks to go with it!

—Wendy Claire Barrie
Director of Children, Youth, and Family Ministries,
St. Bartholomew's Church, New York City

Building Faith Brick by Brick is a unique way of meeting children where they are and engaging them in God's story. Giving each child LEGO® bricks and a blank canvas, Emily's pedagogy links theology and practicality, encouraging children to wonder aloud about God in their midst. This guide helps both novice and veteran leaders facilitate a new way to imagine scripture and engage the energetic and creative children within and outside our parish walls. With a gentle spirit, Emily encourages and equips children and adults to see Scripture come alive and marvel at God's creation.

—The Rev. Abigail W. Moon
Associate Rector for Christian Education and Outreach,
St John's Episcopal Church, Tallahassee, FL

For the people of Saint Michael and All Angels,
who have allowed me to love them
and share this walk of faith.

For Christina, Suzanne, Cathy, Ana, and Mama,
who have been a cheering squad and sacred circle.

...and for Aberlin and McKenzie,
who have shown me the face of God—more than once.

Table of Contents

NEW TESTAMENT STORIES

The Beginning

Most good ideas spring from a need—often an immediate need. *Building Faith Brick by Brick* (originally called *LEGO® My Bible*...but that led to copyright issues) grew out of an 11th-hour realization that there was a hole in the midweek family programming. Somehow I had overlooked first grade. It was an innocent mistake, since only two first-grade boys were coming on Wednesday evenings. They would be arriving in just a few short hours and I needed to be ready to welcome them.

What I knew *(deeply)* was that one of the boys would engage in nothing unless it was related to *Star Wars* or LEGO® bricks. The question then became, "How do I use this to my advantage?" Since I have two daughters, I know next to nothing about *Star Wars*, so in a pinch I turned to a possible LEGO® connection.

With just an hour to spare, I pooled the entire LEGO® collection from the nursery school, picked a story that seemed right *(Jacob wrestling with God)*, and headed to the classroom to prepare the space. I remember praying over that room (small, without a lot of floor space) and the volunteer leader (surprisingly rigid). It was one of those "Oh God, here we go" type of prayers then I offered it up for God to do something—anything.

The boys were thrilled.

The volunteer felt like a champion.

I was saved.

God was glorified. *(Amen!)*

The combination of God's grace and my creativity melded together into a new way of doing theological reflection. We were reaching into the stories of God while digging deep down into an enormous bin of LEGO® bricks.

A divine pairing indeed.

A Brick-by-Brick Story: Riley

There is always that story, that child, who shows us the face of God. For me that person is Riley (5 years). Riley struggled with creating anything related to the story and had a one-track mind that only wanted to pray for dead dinosaurs. After five weeks of disconnect, something remarkable happened. We gathered as a group for prayer, storytelling, and reflection on the building questions. We looked at suggested images—as we often did—but this time something was wholly and holy different. Riley worked and worked, digging deep into his bucket, clearly on a mission. When it came time to display and discuss his work with me, he proudly presented a tiny creation consisting of three LEGO® pieces. It looked like a tiny clam shell with a single LEGO® figure nestled inside. After five long weeks, Riley slowly spoke the wisdom of the ages, "It is Jonah. The fish wasn't angry. The fish was a helper. This is Jonah and the whale. He was waiting. Waiting for God. Sometimes you need to wait for God, Ms. Emily."

I was standing in the presence of a pint-sized prophet. The Word of God revealed itself in a few plastic pieces. It can happen anywhere if we are willing to show up, be present to our children, and wait for God.

Another Brick-by-Brick Story: Jack

We never know what will bind us together in this life. There are times and moments of connection that happen each day without us realizing their significance. That is, until difficult times come. One of the children from the church I serve walked into the hospital one day with what we thought was a terrible case of growing pains. It turned out that he was beginning a five-month journey through an aggressive and rare form of cancer.

On my way to the hospital, I gathered a healing balm of Pringles, Skittles, and a new set of LEGO® bricks, which, when put together, formed a prehistoric flying bug. I also brought the ridiculously long prayer shawl I had knitted more than six months earlier. I never knew for whom I was knitting until the call came from Jack's family. I suppose it had always been for him.

As I sat by the bedside, it was the language of LEGO® that created a moment of normalcy. Jack and I were talking about how to put the next piece into the prehistoric bug, but what we were really having was Communion. We celebrated a Eucharist of laughter and potato chips that made it clear: God's love is with us—in all times and all places.

A Case for Wondering

We have become a culture that expects prodigies in the halls of elementary schools and professional athletes on the playgrounds. Performance and achievement are in hyper-drive in the lives of many of our children. There isn't a lot of room for dabbling in a few different interests. An "A Team" expectation has taken the place of backyard fun and school-yard free play.

We can find a place to step back from those expectations—children and adults alike. It is time to allow ourselves to enter into a place of wonder—a place of joyful unknowing. It may be scary at first, but that fear can break free into peaceful and fruitful exploration if we make room in our hearts, minds and schedules.

In Bible studies I often say, "I don't know how God really works. If we figured it out, that would make God too small." I truly believe that statement. We can grow in faith and love of God without figuring out the ins and outs of the gifts of grace and the miracle of living. We do not need to perfect life, we need to live it, show up, and enjoy.

How? Open our hands. Unclench our jaws. Step back from the intensity…and wonder. Just wonder. "I don't know" can be one of the most informative and freeing phrases we can utter in our life of faith. Let's help to nurture a generation of God's people who can simply be in the presence of God and wonder.

I have watched the most emotionally unavailable children open like flowers when they have been invited into the process of wondering. I have witnessed the most active children become deeply focused and connected by simply being invited to find their wondering places. There have been truly amazing self-discoveries and theological awakenings around the LEGO®-My-Bible circles. Some of my most treasured time has been being present for "God moments" with children who, in new and renewed ways, access the holy places of their lives. I have no doubt that God continues to show up in really big, important ways. This will happen for your group, too.

The *Building Questions* are the meat of this book. They are the series of wondering questions found in each lesson that are meant to draw us into the stories so we can allow them to transform our lives and inform our living. I have sat at the feet of people like Jerome Berryman, Helen White, Robyn Szoke, David Canan, Jeff Ross, Paul Carling, and Vickie Garvey long enough to witness the power of wonder. I was blessed to be born into a family with Ginny and Charlie Slichter, people who allowed the world to be enormously large and lovingly small. What kind of place will you create so that those around you can flourish and explore?

Note: Several of the lessons repeat the same questions over and over. This is intentional. In each record of faith told in the Bible, we can't ask too many questions about why it matters and how we are a part of the story. Many themes are related, and therefore asking the questions over and over can create a natural connection and continuum for our faith stories. God speaks to us in an epic love story. These stories are for all people. I believe these questions can be pulled out and used in Biblical exploration by all ages—with or without the LEGO® bricks. They can help almost any group to break open Scripture together. Use the questions in this book with your vestry, women's groups, youth gatherings, worship services, sermon writing sessions, and more. We can all make a place in our lives for wonder as we allow the open space to come closer, to simply listen to ourselves and others. The *Building Questions* create a place of greater community and deeper level of trust. In the questions, we come to know one another and God more fully.

Wonder.

Just wonder.

A Few Words about Boy Faith

There is a rather vast, uncharted territory called "boy faith." As faith formers, it is rare that we venture into the rough and ragged places where boys live, learn, and grow. What we know is that many places are not set up to meet the needs of the boy heart and mind. At the top of the list often fall school and church. Neither allows the wiggle room that many need to feel accepted and be encouraged to explore.

This isn't really a surprise, right? We all have boys in our lives who keep us active and bring us joy. Yet, if truth be told, they can also take a whole lot of energy from us too. Most of us have been in settings where we beg boys (fidgety and impulsive) to settle down and act like girls (focused and attentive). The true place of ministry is realizing that there is holiness in that impulsive and active nature if we will only take the time to understand.

I happen to have a heart for sharing faith and life stories with elementary school boys, so I needed to figure out a new language for faith expression. After engaging with boys in different settings, I realized that art response was not enough. Craft supplies and talking were not getting to that place of awakening that I knew lay waiting in the hearts of these boys.

You don't have to search very far before the trends in research clearly emerge. Everyone from the local Parent Teacher Association to the Harvard Medical School is talking about the educational and behavioral issues of boys. Not to be overly dramatic, but we have a crisis on our hands; the statistics are startling:

○ 80% of discipline issues in schools are with boys.

- 75% of children receiving special educational services are male.
- Two-thirds of the lowest grades are "earned" by boys.
- Boys are often evaluated as being up to a year and a half behind their female counterparts by school testing standards.

I have to believe that our boys are not "broken," but the system might be.

The work of Michael Gurian (The Gurian Institute) has captured my attention. He is part of a group looking at the brain-based approach to gender. The concept is relatively new (1990), yet seems to be grounded in intuitive knowledge we have sensed for a long, long time:

- Movement energizes and motivates boys.
- Boys often have a stronger grasp on spatial and mechanical workings.
- Generally, boys respond better to visual cues.

Why? *Brain chemistry*. Chemicals like serotonin truly do affect the manner in which we function. What can we do about this hardwired reality? Begin by acknowledging that there are real learning and behavioral differences between boys and girls. These differences are not better or worse—just different. Understanding this reality informs the way we teach (and learn from) both boys and girls. This understanding helps us make a place for all children to enter into a life of wondering and loving God.

There are many ways this can happen. For me? I finally found a place where real life meets faith sharing: LEGO® bricks...and lots of them. This might be the link you and the children have been seeking.

Finding Your Own Words: The Gift of Retelling the Story

I love to listen to stories just as much as I love to tell them. Our Holy Scripture has deep roots in a shared oral tradition. Reading directly from the Bible is completely fine. Riley's spiritual connection with the Jonah story was the result of a time I read directly from a children's Bible. We were given the written words for our devotion and use, and sometimes the nature of the story, or the time you have, make reading directly the best option.

If you want to make the story sharing more familiar, try telling it in your own words. It is a wonderful gift to each other when we take written stories, learn them, and are able to retell them by heart. This does not mean memorization. It also does not mean taking unnecessary or wacky creative license. It *does* mean placing your heart and words into the center of the circle so the group gathered can get a little closer to God through your sharing.

Tips for Enriching the Sharing of Each Story:
- Spend time in study and reflection.
- Read and reread in preparation. Scripture can speak to us differently each time we open it.
- Keep in mind the age of the group and subject matter in order to tune the length and content accordingly.
- Take into account the learning styles of the group and provide avenues for as many styles as possible.
- Trust children to hear the whole story of God. Avoid the temptation to "water down" the uncomfortable parts of the Bible.

○ Talk to others about what they know or remember about a story from their childhood. If you take yourself back to the place of youthful discovery, you may find the scripture breaks open in a different way.

○ Read both chapter/verse Bible translations and picture Bibles.

○ Write down a few key words or phrases to help you (if needed).

○ Be gentle with yourself. There are many ways to share the stories of God. Don't get caught up in thinking there is only one right way. God is still speaking—through you.

Reading Scripture with Children

Let's be honest. Children are often more open to the words and messages of Scripture than adults. Children have yet to "unlearn" the wonder and joy of the stories. They have no need to pin down facts and poke holes in the imaginative process to protect themselves. Children can allow for the stories to just be what they are and take them as their own.

Adults, on the other hand, can get far too mixed up in the need to prove or disprove, then believe or disbelieve, until they have put the ways of God into a box big enough to love but small enough to figure out.

We can take cues from our children. Let God be God without qualifiers.

Where do I see this the most? The writings attributed to Moses. Children's Bibles (too often) slice and dice these stories to make them less messy and certainly less violent or scandalous. My answer: trust children. If they are in solid and caring relationships with adults who want them to learn and process the messages God is communicating, children will be just fine.

When it comes to the literal or figurative nature of Scripture, there is a lot of room. Depending on when and how we were formed as Christians, we can find ourselves at a number of different points on a continuum. If we look at books like Genesis, it is easy to get caught up in the details. Was it really six days of work and one of rest? Were Adam and Eve actual people? Were all types of animals really in the ark? What about the dinosaurs? How could people really live to be that old? If God loved those people, why wasn't it easier?

The answers might be complex, but the important point is, "Why does it matter?" The important work for us is noticing how the entire arc of the story speaks into our lives. God creates. God loves. God calls people to come closer again and again. God has inspired people of every generation to write down and share the stories of our common faith.

Here is the best part—*all of us continue to be a part of God's story.*

This is not a call to abandon biblical scholarship. Rather, it is a call to invite children into the process of digging deeper and learning what many voices have to say. To the best of our knowledge, there were several writers of the book we know as Genesis. This doesn't take away from the importance of Moses. It actually means that enough people thought the writings were important enough to add their wisdom and knowledge about the history of the Hebrew people. People have agendas and certain slants. The Bible writers were really no different than us. The key to remember is that God uses us all, no matter our perspective.

The Building Faith Brick by Brick Method

General Guidelines

Age Range
○ *Building Faith Brick by Brick* is ideal for children kindergarten through fifth grade.

Group Size
○ *Building Faith Brick by Brick* groups can effectively range from three to 20 children.
○ The adult to child ratio should be at least one adult to every eight children.

Note: Groups can span into adulthood, but pre-kindergarten (age 5) or kindergarten is the youngest age range I have found to be successful and meaningful.

Potential Settings
Building Faith Brick by Brick is appropriate for use in a variety of settings, including, but not limited to:
○ Sunday school curriculum (30 minutes or more)
○ alternative to lesson options found in other curricula (15 minutes or more)
○ after school program (1 hour or more)
○ weekday club (1 hour or more)
○ family or cross-generational event (1 hour or more)
○ retro youth group activity (20 minutes or more)
○ VBS curriculum or supplement (1 hour or more)
○ childcare room option (open ended)
○ home and family devotional (open ended)

Preparation

Story Selection
○ The best stories tend to include action, adventure, battles, drama, wonder, mystery, and/or suspense.
○ Ask for suggestions from the children during the first session. You may be wonderfully surprised by what is suggested.
○ Provide a mix of well-known and obscure stories to provide intrigue as well as to build biblical literacy.
○ Explore only one story each session.
○ Remember to think about the context of the story.
○ Select a child-friendly translation of the Bible—picture or chapter/verse.
○ Use the same Bible for the entire span of sessions. This helps to reinforce that all of the stories can be found in Scripture.

Preparing the Space and Setting the Tone
○ Pray over the space.
○ Clear the room to maximize floor space. "LEGO®ing" is best done on the floor.
○ Place a Christ candle in the room. (It can be a good quality battery powered candle if you are concerned about safety.)
○ Create a place of prayer—akin to "circle time."
○ Place the Bible and samples of story artwork (completed LEGO® structures) in the circle where the leader will sit.
○ Establish a display and discussion space. A table or counter works best.
○ Set up a snack area. Eating family style promotes conversation.
○ Prepare participant supplies. See What Do I Really Need? on page 16 for more details.

Basic Lesson Plan

Welcome the Group

○ Shoes may be removed and lined up along the wall in the hallway. Some children with sensory issues may not wish to remove their shoes, so make shoe removal optional.

○ Welcome each child into the room by an adult volunteer or leader.

○ Provide nametags if you do not know all the participants. The use of names is so important. It also helps children to learn one another's names.

○ Give a bowl/bucket, building mat, and a few figures to each child.

○ Invite each child to fill his/her bowl/bucket with LEGO® bricks and encourage each to create freely while others arrive.

○ Give a 2-minute notice before the focused group time begins.

Note: To avoid mix-ups with bowls, use a dry erase marker to label each bowl/bucket with the group member's name. After trying a number of different styles and shapes, the large, square popcorn buckets available at dollar stores seem to work the best.

Lay the Foundation

○ Each lesson provides background information for both the leader and the group. Details about that lesson's story include authorship, placement in scripture, main characters, and modern day parallels.

Did You Know?

○ This section offers additional background information to spark interest and provide a wider base of knowledge and context before sharing the story. As necessary, tailor the information to the particular age.

Pray

○ Light the Christ candle and pocket the matches.

○ Invite each person voluntarily into some form of prayer:

— Write or draw prayers on brightly colored paper rectangles to build a brick prayer wall session by session.

— Write or draw prayers on Etch-a-Sketches®.

— Write or draw prayers on white boards.

— Toss a LEGO® brick into a central bucket for each prayer offered during the circle gathering. These prayers can be guided or spontaneous.

— Write prayers using magnetic letters placed on metal sheeting or baking trays.

— Offer popcorn prayers: Children pop up to offer a short prayer when so moved.

— Offer Post-It® prayers: Colorful self-adhesive notes can be stuck to the wall to build an ongoing prayer corner.

Share the Story

- ○ Introduce the story by answering some or all of the following questions, as appropriate. Each lesson includes brief answers to most or all of these questions; you are always free to supplement this information from your own knowledge and research:
  - — Where is this story found in the Bible?
  - — What other stories can be found before and after this story?
  - — Who wrote this story?
  - — When did this story take place?
  - — When was the story written?
  - — Whom are we going to "meet" in this story?
  - — Where did this story take place?
  - — Where is this location in today's world?
- ○ Share the story by reading or retelling it.
- ○ Show different images of the story to help spark imagination (art books, original LEGO® constructions, online image sites, etc.).

Respond to the Story
Ask Building Questions

- ○ Allow time for *Building Questions*, comments, and insights. We provide a robust list of questions for each lesson. This time of "wondering" typically serves as the most sacred part of the gathering; try not to rush through the reflections. At this point the interior life of the group often emerges in remarkable ways. This is where the bulk of the theological reflection can be heard and witnessed.
  - ○ The list of *Building Questions* is intentionally longer than needed for any given session so that the lessons can be repeated with the same group over time. This also allows for the leader to pick and choose which question fits best within the context.
- ○ Set the expectation that something from the story must be constructed before any other creations can be made.
- ○ Be available to answer questions, review the story, or help "stuck" children.

Suggest Blueprints

- ○ *Building Faith Brick by Brick* is intended to be an open-ended theological reflection using LEGO® bricks. The need to specifically script a response should be avoided. However, if a child is having a difficult time focusing in on a response to the story, a few suggested idea starters have been offered, called *Blueprints*. The suggestions should only be introduced as needed. Reading *Blueprints* to the whole group could hinder the creative process, so keep them for "as needed" moments.
- ○ Allow the suggested *Blueprints* to be simple words or concepts to spark ideas within the imagination of the child.

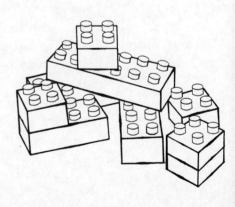

Share Responses

- ○ As children complete their creations, provide a place for temporary display.
- ○ Listen to the stories the children want to share about their work. This can be one on one, or as a whole group, or both ways.
- ○ *Optional:* Take a photo of child with the creation or of the creation alone.

Share a Snack
(optional, but highly recommended)

- ○ Begin or end with a story-related snack, if possible.
- ○ As you snack, check in with each other. Give children the opportunity to tell something new about their lives since the last session. Possible prompts include "Tell me something from your day" and "Tell me something that I would never know unless you told me."
- ○ Pray over the food and the gathered group. This prayer can be led by adults or children and can be a wonderful place to help everyone exercise the art of praying aloud in groups.

Continue the Story

- ○ Encourage each child to show his/her work to a parent/adult and share something from the story or creative process.
- ○ Allow families to explore the story at home by emailing, texting, or making a take-home sheet with the Bible verse.
- ○ If possible, keep creations on display during the week in a location seen by other parts of the faith community.

Frequently Asked Questions

How do I get enough LEGO® pieces?

To experience the full range of creativity, it is helpful to have large quantities of LEGO® pieces. Possible sources are:

- ○ Borrow a supply from an on-site children's program (preschool, daycare, or school).
- ○ Ask for hand-me-downs from families with children aging out of LEGO® bricks.
- ○ Scout tag sales and thrift shops (and ask others in the church to do the same).
- ○ Visit online auction sites.
- ○ Make use of online recycling and swapping sites.
- ○ Request donations of LEGO® bricks or money tagged to purchase them. If you are asking for donations, be specific about the size of LEGO® pieces you desire.
- ○ Take advantage of seasonal sales and store coupons.

Do girls like Building Faith Brick by Brick?

Yes, girls also respond to the art of spiritual LEGO®ing. I have had girls in most of the groups and they have always come back for more. Even if girls aren't in the group, it is still very important to present female stories of the Bible.

How do I help children avoid the temptation to make unrelated creations?

Careful selection of the story helps to keep the focus on what is presented that day. Stories must have obvious characters and plots that are easy to follow. It is also helpful for volunteers to informally move through the room reminding the group of the need to create a response to the story *before* they move on to other, unrelated creation. Gentle redirection can take the form of "Tell me how this creation is connected to the story?" or "What could you make that reminds you of the story we just heard?" It is also good to have a "no gun" or no non-biblical weapon policy.

What do I really need?

- ○ Lots of extra body parts/people/figures. (Visit www.lego.com or your local retailer for currently available parts.)
- ○ A bowl/bucket for each child.
- ○ Baseplates for each child. These help to stretch out the options for creating a whole story scene and not just a few small pieces. LEGO® offers several options. (Visit www.lego.com or your local retailer for currently available parts.)
- ○ Snacks. Powerful conversations seem to happen over food.
- ○ A Bible with a good, engaging translation. See the recommendations on the next page.

Who makes the best volunteers?

The truth is that we work with the resources we have at any given moment. I have found that it is often a mix of abundance and scarcity. Never fear, God can do amazing things through any one of us. If you have the gift of options, here are some qualities you want to encourage in the people you invite in participation and leadership:

- Flexible and creative
- Open to noise and a fair amount of organized chaos
- Do not have a child in the group
- Have a fairly good knowledge of Scripture and are able to field questions
- Physically able to get down on the floor (and get back up again!). If key volunteers have physical limitation, it is possible to move the creative process to tables.

What translations do I use for study, reflection, and group use?

For study and reflection:

- *Harper-Collins Study Bible: New Revised Standard Version Bible*
- *Common English Bible*
- *The Amplified Bible*
- *New American Standard Bible*
- *The Message*
- *The Story: Teen Edition*
- *New International Version*

For Use in Group:

- *The Spark Story Bible*
- *Common English Bible*
- *The Message*

Note: You may stumble across some biblically inaccurate "junk" out there. Be careful! If you are unsure which what Bible to use, ask a trusted person—lay or ordained.

Bibliographic info for recommended Bible translations:

- Meeks, Wayne A., and Jouette M. Bassler. *The HarperCollins Study Bible: New Revised Standard Version, with the Apocryphal/Deuterocanonical Books*. New York, NY: HarperCollins, 1993.
- *Common English Bible: A Fresh Translation to Touch the Heart and Mind*. Nashville: Abingdon, 2010.
- Siewert, Frances E. *The Amplified Bible*. Grand Rapids: Zondervan Pub. House, 1985.
- *The Holy Bible: New American Standard Bible*. New York: American Bible Society, 1991.
- Peterson, Eugene H. *The Message*. Colorado Springs, CO: NavPress, 2004.
- *The Story: The Bible as One Continuing Story of God and His People: Selections from the New International Version*. Grand Rapids, Mich: Zondervan, 2011.
- *The Holy Bible: New International Version*. Colorado Springs, CO: International Bible Society, 1984.
- Arthur, Patti Thisted., Peter Grosshauser, and Ed Temple. *Spark Story Bible*. Minneapolis: Augsburg Fortress, 2009.

The Six Days of Creation:
The First of Two Creation Stories
Genesis 1:1–2:4

Welcome the Group

Lay the Foundation

○ *Where is this story found in the Bible?*
Old Testament

○ *What is its place in the Bible story?*
first story of the Bible, before Cain and Abel

○ *Who is the author?*
Moses and others *(Some scholars believe three or more people helped to write the book we call Genesis.)*

○ *Who are the main characters?*
Adam, Eve, and God

○ *Where in the biblical world did it happen?*
everywhere!

○ *Where is this in today's world?*
everywhere!

Find the full description of *Lay the Foundation* on page 15.

Did You Know?

✔ The word *Genesis* comes from the Greek word for "beginning" or "to be born."

✔ The word *Eden* comes from the Aramaic word for "fruitful" or "well watered."

✔ There are two stories of creation in the Bible.

Pray

Dear God, you are the creator and lover of all things and all people. Thank you for the many creations you have made in this world and in our lives. We ask you to help us to use them in right ways and to your glory. Amen.

Suggested prayer methods are outlined on page 15.

Share the Story

Suggestions for storytelling are detailed on page 16.

Respond to the Story

Invite each member of the group to use bricks and figures to respond to the story. This can be done individually or in small groups. Suggestions for how to support this form of theological reflection can be found on page 16.

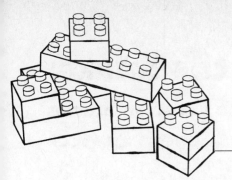

Ask Building Questions

- ◯ I wonder what it felt like in the darkness?
- ◯ I wonder why God didn't create the world all at one time?
- ◯ I wonder what it was like to see the first light?
- ◯ I wonder what the earth smelled like when it was new?
- ◯ I wonder if God ever made anything God thought wasn't good?
- ◯ I wonder if there is anything that God forgot to create?
- ◯ I wonder what part of creation was God's favorite?
- ◯ I wonder what part of creation is your favorite?
- ◯ I wonder if God is finished creating things?
- ◯ I wonder what things we can create with God's help?
- ◯ I wonder what God does to rest?
- ◯ I wonder what it means to be created in the image of God?
- ◯ I wonder how we are like God?

Suggest Blueprints *(if needed)*

- ◯ God
- ◯ darkness
- ◯ water
- ◯ land
- ◯ animals
- ◯ birds
- ◯ water creatures
- ◯ creepy crawlies
- ◯ day
- ◯ night
- ◯ stars
- ◯ heaven
- ◯ rest
- ◯ the first people

Share Responses

Encourage each group member to share the creations they have made in response to the story. More details about sharing can be found on page 17.

Share a Snack

- ◯ blue gelatin with candy fish
- ◯ graham cracker "dirt" crumbles with gummy worms
- ◯ animal crackers
- ◯ goldfish
- ◯ rice cereal treats or cookies in shape of stars, moon, animals, birds, or insects

Continue the Story

One way to deepen the learning experience and create a link between group learning and faith formation in the home is to have builders show their creations to the adults who pick them up after class.

For additional study and conversation at home, consider different ways to share the Bible verses as well as some of the *Building Questions*. Possible methods of communication are texts, social media, e-blasts, website posts, and take-home sheets.

Adam, Eve, and the Snake:
The Second of the Two Creation Stories
Genesis 2:4–3:24

Welcome

Lay the Foundation

○ *Where is this story found in the Bible?*
Old Testament

○ *What is its place in the Bible story?*
after the seven days of creation; before Cain and Abel

○ *Who is the author?*
Moses and others (*Some scholars believe three or more people helped to write the book we call Genesis.*)

○ *Who are the main characters?*
Adam, Eve, snake and God

○ *Where in the biblical world did it happen?*
unknown

○ *Where is this in today's world?*
unknown

Find the full description of *Lay the Foundation* on page 15.

Did You Know?

✔ The Bible never mentions that the fruit from the Tree of Knowledge was an apple.

✔ The name *Adam* comes from the Hebrew word for "ground" or "dirt."

Pray

Dear God, thank you for loving us even when we make wrong choices or do things we regret. Help us to always know you are with us in all the places of our lives. Amen.

Suggested prayer methods are outlined on page 15.

Share the Story

Suggestions for storytelling are detailed on page 16.

Respond to the Story

Invite each member of the group to use bricks and figures to respond to the story. This can be done individually or in small groups. Suggestions for how to support this form of theological reflection can be found on page 16.

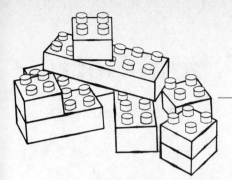

Ask Building Questions

- ○ I wonder why there are two different stories in the Bible about how God created the world?
- ○ I wonder what the breath of God feels like when it touches us?
- ○ I wonder what God used to plant the first garden?
- ○ I wonder what it was like to talk with God?
- ○ I wonder how God dreamt up all of creation?
- ○ I wonder how Adam decided to name the animals?
- ○ I wonder why God didn't want Adam to eat from the Tree of Life?
- ○ I wonder if you have ever done anything you regretted?
- ○ I wonder if you have ever disobeyed anyone?
- ○ I wonder what it would feel like to be naked and not be embarrassed?
- ○ I wonder what it would feel like to be separated from God?
- ○ I wonder what it was like to leave the Garden of Eden?
- ○ I wonder if you have ever felt separated from God?

Suggest Blueprints *(if needed)*

- ○ Adam
- ○ Eve
- ○ garden
- ○ snake
- ○ animals
- ○ God
- ○ outside the garden
- ○ first clothing
- ○ Tree of the Knowledge of Good and Evil

Share Responses to the Story

Encourage group members to share the creations they have made in response to the story. More details about sharing can be found on page 17.

Share a Snack

- ○ green gelatin
- ○ gummy "snakes"
- ○ animal crackers
- ○ fruit
- ○ leaf-shaped cookies
- ○ broccoli "trees" with dip
- ○ graham cracker or cookie "dirt" crumbles with yogurt
- ○ cheese cut with animal shaped cookie cutters

Continue the Story

One way to deepen the learning experience and create a link between group learning and faith formation in the home is to have builders show their creations to the adults who pick them up after class.

For additional study and conversation at home, consider different ways to share the Bible verses as well as some of the *Building Questions*. Possible methods of communication are texts, social media, e-blasts, website posts, and take-home sheets.

Adam, Eve, and the Snake

Cain, Abel, and Seth

Genesis 4:1-26

Welcome the Group

Lay the Foundation

○ *Where is this story found in the Bible?*
Old Testament

○ *What is its place in the Bible story?*
after the fall of Adam and Eve; before Noah

○ *Who is the author?*
Moses and others (*Some scholars believe three or more people helped to write the book we call Genesis.*)

○ *Who are the main characters?*
Cain, Abel, Adam, Eve, Seth, and God

○ *Where in the biblical world did it happen?*
possibly Iran or Iraq

○ *Where is this in today's world?*
possibly Iran or Iraq

Find the full description of *Lay the Foundation* on page 15.

Did You Know?

✔ The name *Abel* means "breath" or "vapor" in Hebrew. This could be because his life was so short lived.

✔ *Cain* means "acquired" in Hebrew.

✔ *Seth* means "appointed one."

✔ This story is the origin of the phrase, "Am I my brother's keeper?"

Pray

God of all people, we thank you for the gift of families. We ask your blessing on our families that they may be a place of love, mercy, and joy. Amen.

Suggested prayer methods are outlined on page 15.

Share the Story

Suggestions for storytelling are detailed on page 16.

Respond to the Story

Invite each member of the group to use bricks and figures to respond to the story. This can be done individually or in small groups. Suggestions for how to support this form of theological reflection can be found on page 16.

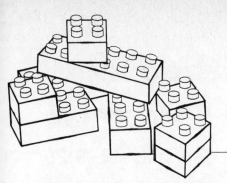

Ask Building Questions

- ○ I wonder if Adam and Eve told their children about the Garden of Eden?
- ○ I wonder why God wasn't pleased with the offering from Cain's flock?
- ○ I wonder what it would feel like if we thought God wasn't pleased with us?
- ○ I wonder what would make someone so angry that s/he would kill someone?
- ○ I wonder how Cain felt after he killed his brother?
- ○ I wonder what God was thinking and feeling when Cain killed Abel?
- ○ I wonder if you have ever been really angry?
- ○ I wonder if you have ever felt that God was angry with you?
- ○ I wonder if you have felt the love of God?
- ○ I wonder what made Adam and Eve want another child?
- ○ I wonder if there is any way to hide from God?
- ○ I wonder if you have ever felt like you wanted to hide from God?
- ○ I wonder if you have ever felt protected by God?

Suggest Blueprints (if needed)

- ○ Cain
- ○ Abel
- ○ Adam
- ○ Eve
- ○ God
- ○ death of Abel
- ○ God talking with Cain
- ○ offerings: meat and vegetables

Share Responses to the Story

Encourage group members to share the creations they have made in response to the story. More details about sharing can be found on page 17.

Share a Snack

- ○ fruit
- ○ vegetables
- ○ rolled meat slices
- ○ beef jerky
- ○ lentil soup
- ○ pita bread and hummus

Continue the Story

One way to deepen the learning experience and create a link between group learning and faith formation in the home is to have builders show their creations to the adults who pick them up after class.

For additional study and conversation at home, consider different ways to share the Bible verses as well as some of the *Building Questions*. Possible methods of communication are texts, social media, e-blasts, website posts, and take-home sheets.

Noah, the Flood, and God's Promise

Genesis 6:1–9:29

Welcome the Group

Lay the Foundation

○ *Where is this story found in the Bible?*
Old Testament

○ *What is its place in the Bible story?*
after Cain, Abel, and Seth; before the Tower of Babel

○ *Who is the author?*
Moses and others *(Some scholars believe three or more people helped to write the book we call Genesis.)*

○ *Who are the main characters?*
Noah, Shem, Ham, Japheth, their wives, animals, and God

○ *Where in the biblical world did it happen?*
Mesopotamia

○ *Where is this in today's world?*
Mount Ararat, Turkey

Find the full description of *Lay the Foundation* on page 15.

Did You Know?

✔ The Bible states that Noah lived to be 950 years old.

✔ A cubit is an ancient measurement roughly equivalent to 18". It was often measured by the length from the top of the forearm to the tip of one's fingers.

✔ The ark was described as being 450' long, 45' tall, and 75' wide.

✔ The only two times the Bible uses the Hebrew word *teba* is for Noah's ark and baby Moses' basket set afloat in the Nile.

Pray

Dear God, who loves and cares for all creation, help us to always be gentle and loving when it comes to the earth. Show us the right ways to live, and how to be thankful for all you have created. Your beauty and wonder is more than we can even imagine. Thank you, God. Amen.

Suggested prayer methods are outlined on page 15.

Share the Story

Suggestions for storytelling are detailed on page 16.

Respond to the Story

Invite each member of the group to use bricks and figures to respond to the story. This can be done individually or in small groups. Suggestions for how to support this form of theological reflection can be found on page 16.

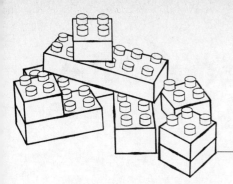

Ask Building Questions

○ I wonder how God felt to see all the wickedness in the world?

○ I wonder what the voice of God sounded like to Noah?

○ I wonder if you would do something important if God asked you?

○ I wonder if you have ever done something that people thought was strange?

○ I wonder if you have ever been in a large boat?

○ I wonder if you have been near a big body of water?

○ I wonder if God has ever made a promise to you?

○ I wonder what it was like to be closed up in a boat with all those animals?

○ I wonder what it was like to be outside of the boat?

○ I wonder how God showed God's love for the people outside the boat?

○ I wonder if Noah and his family ever questioned their faith in God?

○ I wonder if you have a symbol that reminds you of God?

○ I wonder what symbol you would create if you were God?

○ I wonder how you show you are thankful to God?

Suggest Blueprints (if needed)

○ ark
○ rainbow
○ water
○ flood world
○ storms
○ mountain

○ Noah and his family
○ animals
○ construction
○ God
○ dove

Share Responses to the Story

Encourage each group member to share the creations they have made in response to the story. More details about sharing can be found on page 17.

Share a Snack

○ pretzel logs
○ animal crackers
○ blue gelatin
○ rainbow colored cookies
○ colored candy to create rainbows
○ graham cracker boats

Continue the Story

One way to deepen the learning experience and create a link between group learning and faith formation in the home is to have builders show their creations to the adults who pick them up after class.

For additional study and conversation at home, consider different ways to share the Bible verses as well as some of the *Building Questions*. Possible methods of communication are texts, social media, e-blasts, website posts, and take-home sheets.

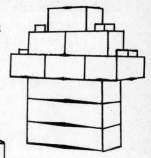

The Tower of Babel
Genesis 11:1-9

Welcome the Group

Lay the Foundation

○ *Where is this story found in the Bible?*
Old Testament

○ *What is its place in the Bible story?*
after Noah; before Abraham and Sarah

○ *Who is the author?*
Moses and others (*Some believe three or more people helped to write the book we call Genesis.*)

○ *Who are the main characters?*
God and the generations of people following the flood

○ *Where in the biblical world did it happen?*
Plain of Shinar

○ *Where is this in today's world?*
Iraq

Find the full description of *Lay the Foundation* on page 15.

Did You Know?

✔ The word *babel* doesn't mean "to talk a lot." (That would be "babble.") It actually is the Hebrew word for "confusion."

Prayer

Dear God, we ask you to make all our words and actions pleasing to you. Teach us how to listen. Help us to build up the kingdom of God and not our own selfish desires. Help us to do our best to understand others different than us, and help us make friendship our goal. Amen.

Suggested prayer methods are outlined on page 15.

Share the Story

Suggestions for storytelling are detailed on page 16.

Respond to the Story

Invite each member of the group to use bricks and figures to respond to the story. This can be done individually or in small groups. Suggestions for how to support this form of theological reflection can be found on page 16.

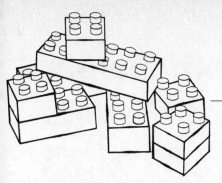

Ask Building Questions

- ○ I wonder if a tower could really reach all the way to heaven?
- ○ I wonder who was the first person to think of making the tower?
- ○ I wonder what the people thought they would see at the top of the tower?
- ○ I wonder what God was thinking as the tower was being built?
- ○ I wonder why the people didn't like living in the small villages?
- ○ I wonder how God thought up all the different languages?
- ○ I wonder what it would feel like if we couldn't understand each other?
- ○ I wonder what it felt like to be at the Tower of Babel?
- ○ I wonder if the unfinished tower is still there today?
- ○ I wonder if you could think of other ways to be close to God?
- ○ I wonder if God has ever come close to you?
- ○ I wonder what we do to try to be too much like God?
- ○ I wonder if kids were allowed to help with building the tower?
- ○ I wonder what the world would be like if everyone spoke the same language?

Suggest Blueprints (if needed)

- ○ tower
- ○ people
- ○ small villages
- ○ tools
- ○ God
- ○ construction site
- ○ big city
- ○ heaven

Share Responses to the Story

Encourage each group member to share the creations they have made in response to the story. More details about sharing can be found on page 17.

Share a Snack

- ○ tower of rice cereal treats
- ○ packs of graham crackers in a tower
- ○ fruit snacks in letter shapes
- ○ tower of pudding or applesauce cups
- ○ gelatin jiggler bricks
- ○ marshmallow "clouds" or building blocks

Continue the Story

One way to deepen the learning experience and create a link between group learning and faith formation in the home is to have builders show their creations to the adults who pick them up after class.

For additional study and conversation at home, consider different ways to share the Bible verses as well as some of the *Building Questions*. Possible methods of communication are texts, social media, e-blasts, website posts, and take-home sheets.

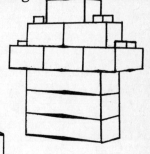

The Tower of Babel

Abraham, Sarah, and the Visitors
Genesis 18:1-15

Welcome the Group
Lay the Foundation

○ *Where is this story found in the Bible?*
Old Testament

○ *What is its place in the Bible story?*
before the destruction of Sodom and Gomorrah; after family struggles between Sarai and Hagar

○ *Who is the author?*
Moses and others (*Some scholars believe three or more people helped to write the book called Genesis.*)

○ *Who are the main characters?*
Abram (*Abraham*), **Sarai** (*Sarah*), **angelic visitors, and God**

○ *Where in the biblical world did it happen?*
trees of Mamre

○ *Where is this in today's world?*
Abraham's life was spent in what is modern day Israel, Jordan and Iraq.

Find the full description of *Lay the Foundation* on page 15.

Did You Know?

✔ Abraham is from the Family of Shem, one of Noah's sons.

✔ God gave Abraham a name change that meant "Father of Many Nations."

✔ Abraham lived to be 175 years old.

Pray

Oh God, your Word is filled with promises and truth. We ask you to come into our lives and create wonder and joy. Help us when we doubt, and be patient when we aren't very patient. Thank you for being with us always. Amen.

Suggested prayer methods are outlined on page 15.

Share the Story

Suggestions for storytelling are detailed on page 16.

Respond to the Story

Invite each member of the group to use bricks and figures to respond to the story. This can be done individually or in small groups. Suggestions for how to support this form of theological reflection can be found on page 16.

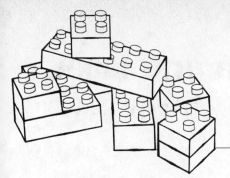

Ask Building Questions

○ I wonder what it would be like to be visited by God?

○ I wonder what it would be like to always live in a tent?

○ I wonder what important people have visited your home?

○ I wonder if you think there is anything too hard even for God to do?

○ I wonder what makes you laugh?

○ I wonder if you remember a time when a baby was born?

○ I wonder if you have heard stories about when you were born?

○ I wonder if God has ever made a promise to you?

Suggest Blueprints *(if needed)*

○ trees
○ tents
○ desert
○ visitors
○ Sarah laughing
○ meal
○ baby

○ Abraham
○ Sarah
○ God

Share Responses to the Story

Encourage each group member to share the creations they have made in response to the story. More details about sharing can be found on page 17.

Share a Snack

○ graham cracker tents
○ party food: bread, cheese, meats, grapes
○ graham cracker sand crumbles over yogurt
○ cottage cheese or string cheese
○ broccoli "trees" with dip

Continue the Story

One way to deepen the learning experience and create a link between group learning and faith formation in the home is to have builders show their creations to the adults who pick them up after class.

For additional study and conversation at home, consider different ways to share the Bible verses as well as some of the *Building Questions*. Possible methods of communication are texts, social media, e-blasts, website posts, and take-home sheets.

Abraham and Isaac
Genesis 22:1-19

Welcome the Group

Lay the Foundation

○ *Where is this story found in the Bible?*
Old Testament
○ *What is its place in the Bible story?*
after God made a promise to Abimelech; before the death of Sarah
○ *Who is the author?*
Moses and others (*Some scholars believe three or more people helped to write the book we call Genesis.*)

○ *Who are the main characters?*
Abraham, Isaac, Sarah, angel, and God
○ *Where in the biblical world did it happen?*
Moriah
○ *Where is this in today's world?*
north of Jerusalem

Find the full description of *Lay the Foundation* on page 15.

Did You Know?

✔ Abraham and Isaac traveled over 50 miles on their trip to the Mount Moriah.

✔ Isaac's name comes from the Hebrew words for "he laughs."

✔ This site in Moriah is thought to be the same location as Solomon's temple, as well as in close proximity to the place where Jesus was crucified.

✔ Most scholars believe Isaac wasn't a child as commonly portrayed. It is possible Isaac was as old as 36 years of age.

Pray

God of mercy and love, help us to listen to your voice in our lives. Help us trust you and honor you this day and always. Amen.

Suggested prayer methods are outlined on page 15.

Share the Story

Suggestions for storytelling are detailed on page 16.

Respond to the Story

Invite each member of the group to use bricks and figures to respond to the story. This can be done individually or in small groups. Suggestions for how to support this form of theological reflection can be found on page 16.

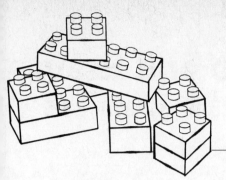

Ask Building Questions

- ❍ I wonder if you have ever heard God call your name?
- ❍ I wonder if you have ever felt tested?
- ❍ I wonder what it is like to hear sad or scary news?
- ❍ I wonder what Abraham was thinking and feeling?
- ❍ I wonder what Isaac was thinking and feeling?
- ❍ I wonder what God was thinking and feeling?
- ❍ I wonder if you have ever been blessed?
- ❍ I wonder if you ever experienced something scary or confusing?
- ❍ I wonder if you have felt the love of God?
- ❍ I wonder if you have given anything special to God?
- ❍ I wonder what would have happened if Abraham refused to follow the directions of God?
- ❍ I wonder if you have felt the protection of God?
- ❍ I wonder if Abraham imagined that you and I are some of the children God promised?

Suggest Blueprints *(if needed)*

- ❍ Abraham
- ❍ Isaac
- ❍ angel
- ❍ Mount Moriah
- ❍ the road they traveled
- ❍ the altar for the sacrifice
- ❍ wood
- ❍ ram
- ❍ God

Share Responses to the Story

Encourage each group member to share the creations they have made in response to the story. More details about sharing can be found on page 17.

Share a Snack

- ❍ "firewood" pretzel sticks
- ❍ hummus and pita bread
- ❍ thin licorice "ropes"
- ❍ star-shaped cookies

Continue the Story

One way to deepen the learning experience and create a link between group learning and faith formation in the home is to have builders show their creations to the adults who pick them up after class.

For additional study and conversation at home, consider different ways to share the Bible verses as well as some of the *Building Questions*. Possible methods of communication are texts, social media, e-blasts, website posts, and take-home sheets.

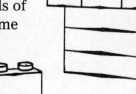

Jacob and Esau
Genesis 25:19-34; 27:1–28:5

Welcome the Group
Lay the Foundation

❍ *Where is this story found in the Bible?*
Old Testament
❍ *What is its place in the Bible story?*
after Isaac married Rebekah; before Jacob wrestled with God
❍ *Who is the author?*
Moses and others (*Some believe three or more people helped to write the book we call Genesis.*)

❍ *Who are the main characters?*
Jacob, Esau, Isaac, Rebekah, and God
❍ *Where in the biblical world did it happen?*
Mesopotamia
❍ *Where is this in today's world?*
Israel

Find the full description of *Lay the Foundation* on page 15.

Did You Know?

✔ Jacob's name comes from the Hebrew words meaning "grab" or "steal." Jacob was holding onto the heel of Esau when they were born.

✔ The name *Esau* can be translated as meaning "red" or "rough," since his body was covered with red hair.

✔ The Bible describes Jacob and Esau as fighting even before Rebekah gave birth to them. She was said to have two warring nations in her womb.

Pray

Dear God, being part of a family is sometimes hard. Show us the goodness in each family member and all those whom we love. Help us to act in ways that show your love in the world. Amen.

Suggested prayer methods are outlined on page 15.

Share the Story

Suggestions for storytelling are detailed on page 16.

Respond to the Story

Invite each member of the group to use bricks and figures to respond to the story. This can be done individually or in small groups. Suggestions for how to support this form of theological reflection can be found on page 16.

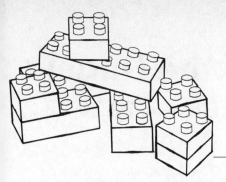

Ask Building Questions

○ I wonder what it is like to want a baby when you aren't able to have one?

○ I wonder if you have ever prayed for something for a really long time?

○ I wonder if you would rather be a hunter or a farmer?

○ I wonder if you have someone who is extra special to you in your family?

○ I wonder if you have ever made a bad choice?

○ I wonder if parents ever make choices they regret?

○ I wonder what it is like to be a twin brother or sister?

○ I wonder who is the most interesting person to you in this story?

○ I wonder if you have ever been so hungry you thought you might die?

○ I wonder if you have ever been really angry with a family member?

○ I wonder what it's like to be near a person who is ready to die?

○ I wonder if you have ever felt tricked by someone?

○ I wonder if you have ever tried to trick someone?

○ I wonder why people want to kill one another?

○ I wonder if you have ever felt like you wanted to run away?

○ I wonder if anyone has ever blessed you?

○ I wonder if you have ever blessed someone?

○ I wonder what a blessing sounds like? feels like?

Suggest Blueprints *(if needed)*

○ Jacob
○ Esau
○ Isaac
○ Rebekah
○ hairy body

○ hunting
○ farming
○ stew
○ blessing
○ God

Share Responses to the Story

Encourage each group member to share the creations they have made in response to the story. More details about sharing can be found on page 17.

Share a Snack

○ meatballs
○ beef jerky
○ lentil soup

○ popsicles
○ bread
○ vegetables

Continue the Story

One way to deepen the learning experience and create a link between group learning and faith formation in the home is to have builders show their creations to the adults who pick them up after class.

For additional study and conversation at home, consider different ways to share the Bible verses as well as some of the *Building Questions*. Possible methods of communication are texts, social media, e-blasts, website posts, and take-home sheets.

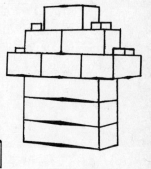

Jacob and the Angel
Genesis 22:24-32

Welcome the Group

Lay the Foundation

○ *Where is this story found in the Bible?*
Old Testament

○ *What is its place in the Bible story?*
after Jacob stole Esau's birthright and blessing; before Jacob was named Israel

○ *Who is the author?*
Moses and others (*Some believe three or more people helped to write the book we call Genesis.*)

○ *Who are the main characters?*
Jacob and God

○ *Where in the biblical world did it happen?*
Bethel

○ *Where is this in today's world?*
Bethel (*10 miles north of Jerusalem*)

Find the full description of *Lay the Foundation* on page 15.

Did You Know?

✓ Jacob's name was changed to *Israel* after he wrestled with God. The name *Israel* means "one who struggles with God and prevails."

✓ Even though Jacob acted like a coward, he became the father of the 12 tribes of Israel.

✓ The name *Bethel* means "House of God" in Hebrew.

Pray

Life is sometimes a struggle, O God. Be with us in the joy and the pain, the laughter and the tears. Help us to know that when you come into our lives, we are never the same. Change us in good ways, give us your wisdom, and call us back to you. Amen.

Suggested prayer methods are outlined on page 15.

Share the Story

Suggestions for storytelling are detailed on page 16.

Respond to the Story

Invite each member of the group to use bricks and figures to respond to the story. This can be done individually or in small groups. Suggestions for how to support this form of theological reflection can be found on page 16.

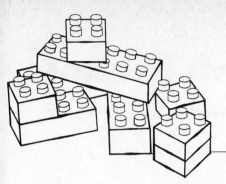

Ask Building Questions

- ○ I wonder if you have ever slept outside?
- ○ I wonder if you have ever struggled with God?
- ○ I wonder what it would be like to be close to an angel?
- ○ I wonder if God has ever come that close to you?
- ○ I wonder what new name would be right for you? for me?
- ○ I wonder who named you?
- ○ I wonder what makes your name special?
- ○ I wonder if God has ever changed you?

Blueprint *(if needed)*

- ○ Jacob
- ○ angel
- ○ God
- ○ wrestling
- ○ outside scene

Share Responses to the Story

Encourage each group member to share the creations they have made in response to the story. More details about sharing can be found on page 17.

Share a Snack

- ○ carrot or celery stick "ladders"
- ○ cotton-candy "clouds"
- ○ marshmallow "rocks"
- ○ popcorn "rocks"

Continue the Story

One way to deepen the learning experience and create a link between group learning and faith formation in the home is to have builders show their creations to the adults who pick them up after class.

For additional study and conversation at home, consider different ways to share the Bible verses as well as some of the *Building Questions*. Possible methods of communication are texts, social media, e-blasts, website posts, and take-home sheets.

Joseph's Dreams
Genesis 39:20–41:36

Welcome the Group
Lay the Foundation

○ *Where is this story found in the Bible?*
Old Testament

○ *What is its place in the Bible story?*
after Joseph's brother sold him into slavery; before Jacob's family moved to Egypt

○ *Who is the author?*
Moses and others (*Some believe three or more people helped to write the book we call Genesis.*)

○ *Who are the main characters?*
Joseph, baker, cupbearer, Pharaoh

○ *Where in the biblical world did it happen?*
Egypt

○ *Where is this in today's world?*
Egypt

Find the full description of *Lay the Foundation* on page 15.

Did You Know?

✔ Joseph was one of 12 brothers.

✔ Joseph was sold into slavery by his jealous brothers when he was about 17 years old.

Pray

Dear God, make us people who forgive others. Make our hearts full and show us the way to live. Help us to listen to you and share your message with others. Amen.

Suggested prayer methods are outlined on page 15.

Share the Story

Suggestions for storytelling are detailed on page 16.

Respond to the Story

Invite each member of the group to use bricks and figures to respond to the story. This can be done individually or in small groups. Suggestions for how to support this form of theological reflection can be found on page 16.

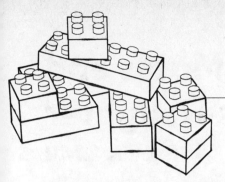

Ask Building Questions

- ○ I wonder if you have ever had a dream you remember?
- ○ I wonder what it would be like if someone could tell you the meaning of your dreams?
- ○ I wonder if you have ever known someone who has been in prison?
- ○ I wonder what Joseph was feeling when he was in prison?
- ○ I wonder if you have ever been given sad and bad news?
- ○ I wonder if you have ever been given happy or exciting news?
- ○ I wonder if you have ever had sad news to share?
- ○ I wonder if you have ever had happy or exciting news to share?
- ○ I wonder if you have felt forgotten?
- ○ I wonder if you have ever been a helper to others?
- ○ I wonder if you have ever been the only one who could understand something?
- ○ I wonder if you ever thought you had a special gift or talent?
- ○ I wonder what special gift or talent God has given you?

- ○ I wonder in what ways God is trying to talk with you?
- ○ I wonder if you have ever wanted to get rid of a brother or sister?

Suggest Blueprints (if needed)

- ○ Joseph
- ○ baker
- ○ butler
- ○ Pharaoh
- ○ cows (fat and skinny)
- ○ grain (healthy and sick)
- ○ prison
- ○ palace

Share Responses to the Story

Encourage each group member to share the creations they have made in response to the story. More details about sharing can be found on page 17.

Share a Snack

- ○ dairy products
- ○ bread
- ○ pasta
- ○ baked goods
- ○ pretzel-rod "prison doors"

Continue the Story

One way to deepen the learning experience and create a link between group learning and faith formation in the home is to have builders show their creations to the adults who pick them up after class.

For additional study and conversation at home, consider different ways to share the Bible verses as well as some of the *Building Questions*. Possible methods of communication are texts, social media, e-blasts, website posts, and take-home sheets.

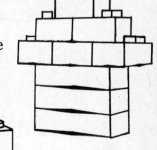

Moses and Pharaoh's Daughter
Exodus 2:1-10

Welcome the Group

Lay the Foundation

○ *Where is this story found in the Bible?*
Old Testament

○ *What is its place in the Bible story?*
after Joseph died; before Moses escaped to Midian

○ *Who is the author?*
Moses and others (*Some believe three or more people helped to write the book we call Exodus.*)

○ *Who are the main characters?*
Moses, Pharaoh, Pharaoh's daughter, Moses' sister, and Moses' mother

○ *Where in the biblical world did it happen?*
Egypt

○ *Where is this in today's world?*
Egypt

Find the full description of *Lay the Foundation* on page 15.

Did You Know?

✔ The word *exodus* comes from the Greek words for "the way out." It details the stories of the Israelites moving from slavery to life in the Promised Land. The journey lasted more than 40 years.

✔ The only two times the Bible uses the Hebrew word *teba* is for Noah's ark and baby Moses' basket set afloat in the Nile.

✔ The name *Moses* is from the Egyptian word for "son" or possibly the Hebrew word for "deliver." It is also said to mean "saved from the water."

Pray

Dear God, we thank you for the many ways we create families. Being part of a family, whether born or chosen, is a gift from you. Thank you for people who adopt children and for those who care for children when others are unable to care for them. Amen.

Suggested prayer methods are outlined on page 15.

Share the Story

Suggestions for storytelling are detailed on page 16.

Respond to the Story

Invite each member of the group to use bricks and figures to respond to the story. This can be done individually or in small groups. Suggestions for how to support this form of theological reflection can be found on page 16.

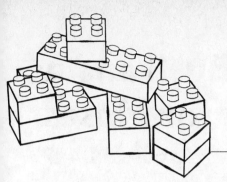

Ask Building Questions

○ I wonder if you have ever been close to a tiny baby?
○ I wonder if anyone has told you stories about when you were a baby?
○ I wonder if you have ever been far away from your family?
○ I wonder what it would be like to take a bath in a river?
○ I wonder if you know anyone who has been adopted?
○ I wonder if you know the special meaning of your name?
○ I wonder why the Pharaoh was afraid of the Hebrew babies?
○ I wonder what it is like to be different from the rest of your family?

Suggest Blueprints *(if needed)*

○ Moses
○ palace
○ babies
○ Pharaoh
○ Pharaoh's daughter
○ Moses' sister
○ Moses' mother
○ Nile River
○ basket

Share Responses to the Story

Encourage each group member to share the creations they have made in response to the story. More details about sharing can be found on page 17.

Share a Snack

○ blue gelatin
○ baskets (cake cups with lattice pastry dough)

Continue the Story

One way to deepen the learning experience and create a link between group learning and faith formation in the home is to have builders show their creations to the adults who pick them up after class.

For additional study and conversation at home, consider different ways to share the Bible verses as well as some of the *Building Questions*. Possible methods of communication are texts, social media, e-blasts, website posts, and take-home sheets.

The Burning Bush and a Helper for Moses

Exodus 3:1-4:17

Welcome the Group

Lay the Foundation

❍ *Where is this story found in the Bible?*
Old Testament

❍ *What is its place in the Bible story?*
after Moses escaped to Midian; before Moses and Aaron went to Pharaoh

❍ *Who is the author?*
Moses and others (*Some scholars believe three or more people helped to write the book we call Exodus.*)

❍ *Who are the main characters?*
Moses, Aaron, God, Israelites, and Pharaoh

❍ *Where in the biblical world did it happen?*
Horeb

❍ *Where is this in today's world?*
Saudi Arabia

Find the full description of *Lay the Foundation* on page 15.

Did You Know?

✔ The word *exodus* comes from the Greek words for "the way out." It details the stories of the Israelites moving from slavery to life in the Promised Land. The journey was more than 40 years.

✔ The distance between Mount Sinai and Egypt is 200 miles.

✔ Some scholars believe that the cause of Moses' fear of speaking and leading the people of Israel was because he was a stutterer.

✔ Since the Egyptians had many gods, Moses wanted to know the name of God because he wanted to be clear that his God was the one and only true God.

✔ The name *Moses* is from the Egyptian word for "son" or possibly the Hebrew word for "deliver." It is also said to mean "saved from the water."

Pray

Holy One, set our hearts on fire with love and joy. Help us to listen for your voice in all the places of our lives, and call us to do amazing things in this world. Amen.

Suggested prayer methods are outlined on page 15.

Share the Story

Suggestions for storytelling are detailed on page 16.

Respond to the Story

Invite each member of the group to use bricks and figures to respond to the story.

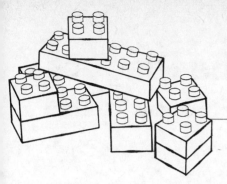

This can be done individually or in small groups. Suggestions for how to support this form of theological reflection can be found on page 16.

Ask Building Questions

○ I wonder what it is like to be a shepherd?
○ I wonder if you have ever seen an angel?
○ I wonder what you would say if God spoke to you?
○ I wonder if you have ever been to a holy place?
○ I wonder what you would do to remember a holy place?
○ I wonder how God can see all things?
○ I wonder what special job you will do for God? *(Maybe you are already doing it.)*
○ I wonder what is your favorite name for God?
○ I wonder what a new name for God could be?
○ I wonder what sign from God would make you brave?
○ I wonder what it would be like to witness a miracle of God?
○ I wonder if you have ever been part of a miracle?
○ I wonder if you know the difference between a miracle and magic?

○ I wonder if the Hebrew people ever felt like God had forgotten them?
○ I wonder if you have ever seen God in an unexpected place?
○ I wonder what it would feel like for God to be angry with you?
○ I wonder what really important things you have said?
○ I wonder if you can think of a time when someone helped you when you really needed help?

Suggest Blueprints *(if needed)*

○ burning bush
○ Moses
○ Aaron
○ God
○ staff that turned into a snake
○ Nile River filled with blood
○ Mount Sinai
○ Hebrew people
○ leprous hand

Share Responses to the Story

Encourage each group member to share the creations they have made in response to the story. More details about sharing can be found on page 17.

Share a Snack

○ red cotton-candy "flames"
○ watermelon cut in bush shapes
○ "mountain" of popcorn

Continue the Story

One way to deepen the learning experience and create a link between group learning and faith formation in the home is to have builders show their creations to the adults who pick them up after class.

For additional study and conversation at home, consider different ways to share the Bible verses as well as some of the *Building Questions*. Possible methods of communication are texts, social media, e-blasts, website posts, and take-home sheets.

The Plagues
Exodus 7:1–11:10

Welcome the Group

Lay the Foundation

❍ *Where is this story found in the Bible?*
Old Testament

❍ *What is its place in the Bible story?*
after Aaron was called as Moses' helper; before the Exodus of the Israelites

❍ *Who is the author?*
Moses and others *(Some scholars believe three or more people helped to write the book we call Exodus.)*

❍ *Who are the main characters?*
Moses, Aaron, Pharaoh, Magicians, Israelites, and God

❍ *Where in the biblical world did it happen?*
Egypt

❍ *Where is this in today's world?*
Egypt

Find the full description of *Lay the Foundation* on page 15.

Did You Know?

✔ The word *exodus* comes from the Greek words for "the way out." It details the stories of the Israelites moving from slavery to life in the Promised Land. The journey was more than 40 years.

Prayer

Dear God, help us to always remember that you are with us no matter what is happening. Keep us focused on your love, and let us feel your protection. Amen.

Suggested prayer methods are outlined on page 15.

Share the Story

Suggestions for storytelling are detailed on page 16.

Note: Depending on the age of your group, the story of the plagues can be a bit lengthy to read directly from the Bible. This may be the perfect time to tell the story in place of reading it. It is one of those stories that children's Bibles generally tell poorly. I suggest you really look at the story in a chapter-verse Bible to get the full details and important nuances. I believe children have the ability to understand the challenging and (sometimes) disturbing stories of the Bible. I encourage you to resist the urge to "water it down" or avoid the tough parts of our faith narrative. Processing is key.

Respond to the Story

Invite each member of the group to use bricks and figures to respond to the story. This can be done individually or in small groups.

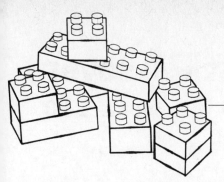

Suggestions for how to support this form of theological reflection can be found on page 16.

Ask Building Questions

- ○ I wonder if you have ever had an important message to tell someone?
- ○ I wonder if you can tell the difference between magic and a miracle?
- ○ I wonder if you have ever had a time when someone refused to listen to you?
- ○ I wonder if the Pharaoh was ever afraid?
- ○ I wonder if you have you ever made a deal with someone?
- ○ I wonder if anything has happened in nature that made you afraid?
- ○ I wonder why God continued to harden the heart of Pharaoh?
- ○ I wonder if you have ever had to harden your heart?
- ○ I wonder if you ever tried to soften your heart?
- ○ I wonder if you have known anyone who breaks his/her promises?
- ○ I wonder if you have ever felt like you couldn't get away from someone?
- ○ I wonder if you have ever cried out to God?
- ○ I wonder how it would feel if you weren't allowed to worship God?
- ○ I wonder if you have ever wondered about God's love?

Suggest Blueprints *(if needed)*

- ○ Pharaoh
- ○ Aaron
- ○ Moses
- ○ people of Egypt
- ○ Israelites
- ○ sorcerers
- ○ staff as serpent
- ○ Nile River
- ○ Nile River of blood
- ○ frogs
- ○ gnats (bugs)
- ○ flies
- ○ livestock
- ○ boils
- ○ hail
- ○ locusts
- ○ darkness
- ○ death

Share Responses to the Story

Encourage each group member to share the creations they have made in response to the story. More details about sharing can be found on page 17.

Share a Snack

- ○ red gelatin
- ○ grasshopper cookies
- ○ insect-shaped fruit snacks or gummy candies
- ○ pudding colored with red dye
- ○ pretzel rod "staffs"
- ○ frozen grape or blueberry "hail" *(Beware of choking hazard.)*
- ○ red fruit roll strips for the bloody Nile River
- ○ popcorn for hail

Continue the Story

One way to deepen the learning experience and create a link between group learning and faith formation in the home is to have builders show their creations to the adults who pick them up after class.

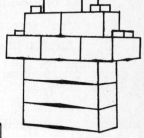

For additional study and conversation at home, consider different ways to share the Bible verses as well as some of the *Building Questions*. Possible methods of communication are texts, social media, e-blasts, website posts, and take-home sheets.

The First Passover

Exodus 12:1-28

Welcome the Group

Lay the Foundation

○ *Where is this story found in the Bible?*
Old Testament

○ *What is its place in the Bible story?*
after the plagues in Egypt; before the Exodus

○ *Who is the author?*
Moses and others (*Some scholars believe three or more people helped to write the book we call Exodus.*)

○ *Who are the main characters?*
Moses, Aaron, Angel, Pharaoh, Egyptians, Israelites, and God

○ *Where in the biblical world did it happen?*
Egypt

○ *Where is this in today's world?*
Egypt

Find the full description of *Lay the Foundation* on page 15.

Did You Know?

✔ The term *Passover* comes from God "passing over" the Israelite homes with marked doorposts as told in the Book of Exodus. The blood on the doorposts was a sign to keep them safe from the angel of death while they were still in Egypt.

✔ The word *exodus* comes from the Greek words "the way out." It details the stories of the Hebrew people moving from slavery to life in the Promised Land. The journey was more than 40 years.

Pray

Holy God, you have been the protector of people since the beginning of time. Thank you for loving us and giving us life. You are a God who waves a hand of mercy and peace over our lives. Help us to remember your goodness and compassion. Amen.

Suggested prayer methods are outlined on page 15.

Share the Story

Suggestions for storytelling are detailed on page 16.

Respond to the Story

Invite each member of the group to use bricks and figures to respond to the story. This can be done individually or in small groups. Suggestions for how to support this form of theological reflection can be found on page 16.

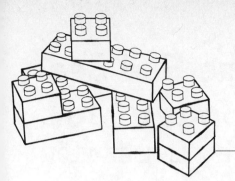

Ask Building Questions

○ I wonder what special traditions you have with your friends and family?

○ I wonder what ways you might remember God's love with your friends and family?

○ I wonder if you have ever shared a holy meal with someone?

○ I wonder if God has ever talked to you?

○ I wonder if you have ever been close to an angel?

○ I wonder what you like to wear for important gatherings?

○ I wonder if you have ever eaten in a hurry?

○ I wonder if you have a sign or symbol in your house that shows your love for God?

○ I wonder if you have ever needed to follow a rule that you didn't understand?

○ I wonder if you have ever felt the protection of someone who loves you?

Suggest Blueprints *(if needed)*

○ God
○ Moses
○ Aaron
○ Israelites
○ Egyptians
○ doors with blood on lintels and doorposts
○ hurried meal
○ fire
○ lamb
○ angel
○ children

Share Responses to the Story

Encourage each group member to share the creations they have made in response to the story. More details about sharing can be found on page 17.

Share a Snack

○ cookie "doors" with jelly "blood"
○ lamb or other meat
○ pita bread, matzo, tortillas, or other unleavened bread
○ traditional foods served for Passover: hard boiled eggs, herbs dipped in salt water, red grape juice, apple-nut paste *(charoset)*, lettuce, and horseradish

Continue the Story

One way to deepen the learning experience and create a link between group learning and faith formation in the home is to have builders show their creations to the adults who pick them up after class.

For additional study and conversation at home, consider different ways to share the Bible verses as well as some of the *Building Questions*. Possible methods of communication are texts, social media, e-blasts, website posts, and take-home sheets.

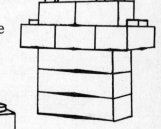

Parting of the Red Sea and Songs of Joy

Exodus 13:17–15:21

Welcome the Group

Lay the Foundation

○ *Where is this story found in the Bible?*
Old Testament

○ *What is its place in the Bible story?*
after the first Passover; before God provided manna and quail

○ *Who is the author?*
Moses and others (*Some scholars believe three or more people helped to write the book we call Exodus.*)

○ *Who are the main characters?*
Moses, Aaron, Miriam, Israelites, Pharaoh, Egyptians, and God

○ *Where in the biblical world did it happen?*
Red Sea

○ *Where is this in today's world?*
Red Sea (*between the Arabian Peninsula and Africa*)

Find the full description of *Lay the Foundation* on page 15.

Did You Know?

✔ The word *exodus* comes from the Greek words for "the way out." This is the beginning of the story where Moses and God's people wandered in the desert for forty years.

✔ Over 600,000 men traveled with Moses. There were also untold numbers of women, children and non-Israelites journeying with the men.

✔ Moses carried the bones of Joseph with him so Joseph wouldn't be buried in Egypt.

✔ The name *Red Sea* is possibly a mistranslation of the Hebrew word for "reed" and not the color red. The water in that body of water was filled with reeds.

Pray

Oh God, just as you parted the waters for the Hebrew people, we trust you can perform miracles even today. Remind us to look for the goodness of your grace, and help to expect wonderful things. Teach us to trust in your power and love. Let us rejoice in you each day. Amen.

Suggested prayer methods are outlined on page 15.

Share the Story

Suggestions for storytelling are detailed on page 16.

Respond to the Story

Invite each member of the group to use bricks and figures to respond to the story. This can be done individually or in small groups. Suggestions for how to support this

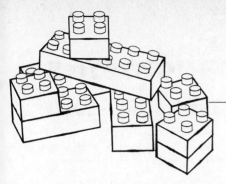

form of theological reflection can be found on page 16.

Ask Building Questions

- ○ I wonder what God was saying to Pharaoh?
- ○ I wonder why it is called the "Red Sea"?
- ○ I wonder if you have ever followed a sign from God?
- ○ I wonder if you have ever changed your mind about something big and important?
- ○ I wonder if you have ever been really afraid?
- ○ I wonder if you have ever seen God in a cloud? in fire?
- ○ I wonder where you would follow God?
- ○ I wonder if you have ever been a part of a miracle?
- ○ I wonder if you have ever been confused by God? by people?
- ○ I wonder if you have ever known a really good leader?
- ○ I wonder if you have been a leader?
- ○ I wonder if you have ever cried out for God?
- ○ I wonder if you have ever been near a big body of water?

○ I wonder if you have ever been so happy that you wanted to sing and dance?
○ I wonder what song you would write for God?

Suggest Blueprints *(if needed)*

- ○ pillar of fire
- ○ pillar of cloud
- ○ Moses
- ○ Pharaoh
- ○ Pharaoh's army (Egyptians)
- ○ parted water
- ○ God
- ○ Joseph's bones
- ○ Israelites
- ○ chariots

Share Responses to the Story

Encourage each group member to share the creations they have made in response to the story. More details about sharing can be found on page 17.

Share a Snack

- ○ marshmallow cloud "pillars"
- ○ fish crackers
- ○ blue and green gelatin jigglers that can stack up to make the parted water
- ○ gummy fish
- ○ cookie crumble "dry land"
- ○ chariot "wagon wheel" pasta
- ○ pretzel rod "pillars" with red shoestring "flames"

Continue the Story

One way to deepen the learning experience and create a link between group learning and faith formation in the home is to have builders show their creations to the adults who pick them up after class.

For additional study and conversation at home, consider different ways to share the Bible verses as well as some of the *Building Questions*. Possible methods of communication are texts, social media, e-blasts, website posts, and take-home sheets.

The Ten Commandments
Exodus 19:1–20:21

Welcome the Group

Lay the Foundation

○ *Where is this story found in the Bible?*
Old Testament

○ *What is its place in the Bible story?*
after God gave manna, quail, and water to the Israelites; before God gave instructions for the Ark of the Covenant (box) and a Tabernacle (tent)

○ *Who is the author?*
Moses and others (*Some scholars believe three or more people helped to write the book we call Exodus.*)

○ *Who are the main characters?*
Moses, Aaron, Israelites, and God

○ *Where in the biblical world did it happen?*
Mount Sinai

○ *Where is this in today's world?*
the Sinai Peninsula (Egypt) or Saudi Arabia

Find the full description of *Lay the Foundation* on page 15.

Did You Know?

✔ The word *Exodus* comes from the Greek words for "the way out." This is the beginning of the story where Moses and God's people wandered in the desert for 40 years.

✔ The Bible mentions two different names for the mountain where Moses met God—Sinai (in Exodus) and Horeb (in Deuteronomy).

✔ There are four commandments about how we should love and honor God as well as six commandments about how to love and care for others.

Pray

Dear God, lead us in the right ways to live. Thank you for the Ten Commandments and the examples of how we should try to be each day. Give us grace when we fall short and help us to remember that your love and mercy are new each day. Amen.

Suggested prayer methods are outlined on page 15.

Share the Story

Suggestions for storytelling are detailed on page 16.

Respond to the Story

Invite each member of the group to use bricks and figures to respond to the story. This can be done individually or in small groups. Suggestions for how to support this form of theological reflection can be found on page 16.

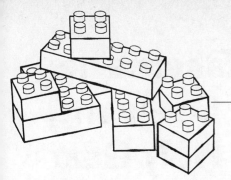

Ask Building Questions

○ I wonder if you have ever felt God's presence?

○ I wonder what it felt like to be on the mountain with God?

○ I wonder if anyone has ever commanded you to do something?

○ I wonder if God is still visiting people?

○ I wonder what important things you have to say?

○ I wonder if you ever feel like you can't get close enough to God?

○ I wonder if you believe there is only one God?

○ I wonder if you think there is something more wonderful than God?

○ I wonder if you ever use words in a way that doesn't honor God?

○ I wonder if you take enough time to rest and thank God?

○ I wonder how you show you are thankful for your family?

○ I wonder if you have ever hurt someone or taken something that doesn't belong to you?

○ I wonder if you have ever said anything that was untrue?

○ I wonder if you have ever wanted more than the things you already own?

○ I wonder why God gave us rules to follow?

○ I wonder if these are the only rules God has for us?

○ I wonder how it feels to try to follow God's rules?

○ I wonder what happens when we don't follow God's rules?

Suggest Blueprints *(if needed)*

○ Mount Sinai

○ Moses

○ Israelites

○ God

○ stone tablets

Share Responses to the Story

Encourage each group member to share the creations they have made in response to the story. More details about sharing can be found on page 17.

Share a Snack

○ rice cereal treat "mountains"

○ pita and hummus

○ marshmallow "smoke" spread on bread or crackers

○ cookie "tablets"

Continue the Story

One way to deepen the learning experience and create a link between group learning and faith formation in the home is to have builders show their creations to the adults who pick them up after class.

For additional study and conversation at home, consider different ways to share the Bible verses as well as some of the *Building Questions*. Possible methods of communication are texts, social media, e-blasts, website posts, and take-home sheets.

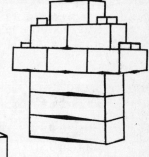

The Tabernacle, Ark of the Covenant, and All the Holy Gear

Exodus 25–30, 35–40

Welcome the Group

Lay the Foundation

❍ *Where is this story found in the Bible?*
Old Testament

❍ *What is its place in the Bible story?*
after the Ten Commandments were given to Moses; before the Israelites worshiped the golden calf

❍ *Who is the author?*
Moses and others (*Some scholars believe three or more people helped to write the book we call Exodus.*)

❍ *Who are the main characters?*
Moses, Aaron, Israelites, and God

❍ *Where in the biblical world did it happen?*
Southern desert of Israel

❍ *Where is this in today's world?*
Southern desert of Israel

Find the full description of *Lay the Foundation* on page 15.

Did You Know?

✔ The word *Exodus*[2] comes from the Greek words for "the way out." This is the beginning of the story where Moses and God's people wandered in the desert for 40 years.

✔ A cubit is approximately 18". It was often measured by the distance from the top of the forearm to the tip of one's finger.

✔ Based on the description in the Bible, the Ark of the Covenant was 45" long, 27" wide and 27" tall.

✔ God's first priests were Levites (descendents of Jacob's son, Levi).

Pray

Dear God, we know that your presence is always around us. Help to us look for you everywhere. Amen.

Suggested prayer methods are outlined on page 15.

Share the Story

Suggestions for storytelling are detailed on page 16.

Note: Since this descriptive portion of scripture is rather long, it might be a good time to tell this story by heart. It has vivid images so it would be a perfect time to show artist renderings to help spur along the creative imagination.

Respond to the Story

Invite each member of the group to use bricks and figures to respond to the story. This can be done individually or in small groups.

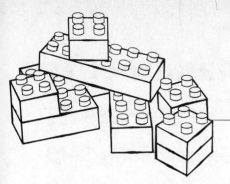

Suggestions for how to support this form of theological reflection can be found on page 16.

Ask Building Questions

○ I wonder what the word *sanctuary* means to you?
○ I wonder where is the holiest place you have ever been?
○ I wonder what you would have brought to the tabernacle to honor God?
○ I wonder why God gave so many details about how to make the Tabernacle and the Ark of the Covenant?
○ I wonder if God really needed all those things?
○ I wonder where it all came from since the Israelites had been slaves for such a long time?
○ I wonder if you have ever needed to sacrifice something for God?
○ I wonder how you prepare to spend time worshiping God?
○ I wonder if you have ever smelled incense?
○ I wonder if you have ever been touched with holy oil?
○ I wonder what is the most treasured/precious thing you have?

○ I wonder if you have a special place where you keep your treasured things?
○ I wonder what you would put on an altar you created for God?
○ I wonder if you have ever thought about being a priest or a deacon?
○ I wonder what other ways people can serve God?

Suggest Blueprints *(if needed)*

○ Ark of the Covenant
○ altar
○ lampstand
○ tabernacle
○ Ten Commandments on two tablets
○ tent
○ courtyard
○ vestments
○ priests

Share Responses to the Story

Encourage each group member to share the creations they have made in response to the story. More details about sharing can be found on page 17.

Share a Snack

○ Creative tent making with Fruit Roll Up® "fabric," crackers, gold and silver decorative baking balls, frosting and other colorful edible items

Continue the Story

One way to deepen the learning experience and create a link between group learning and faith formation in the home is to have builders show their creations to the adults who pick them up after class.

For additional study and conversation at home, consider different ways to share the Bible verses as well as some of the *Building Questions*. Possible methods of communication are texts, social media, e-blasts, website posts, and take-home sheets.

The Ten Commandments Are Given Again
Deuteronomy 9–10

Welcome the Group

Lay the Foundation

○ *Where is this story found in the Bible?*
Old Testament

○ *What is its place in the Bible story?*
after the Ark of the Covenant and the Tabernacle were built; before Aaron died

○ *Who is the author?*
Moses and others (*Some scholars believe three or more people helped to write the book we call Deuteronomy.*)

○ *Who are the main characters?*
Moses, Aaron, Israelites and God

○ *Where in the biblical world did it happen?*
Mt. Horeb

○ *Where is this in today's world?*
Southern desert of Israel

Find the full description of *Lay the Foundation* on page 15.

Did You Know?

✔ The Bible mentions two different names for the mountain where Moses met God—Sinai (in Exodus) and Horeb (in Deuteronomy).

✔ There are four commandments about how we should love and honor God as well as six commandments about how to love and care for others.

Pray

Dear God, we thank you for giving us guidance about the way we should live. Help us to love you and all your children, so that our lives may honor you. Amen.

Suggested prayer methods are outlined on page 15.

Share the Story

Suggestions for storytelling are detailed on page 16.

Respond to the Story

Invite each member of the group to use bricks and figures to respond to the story. This can be done individually or in small groups. Suggestions for how to support this form of theological reflection can be found on page 16.

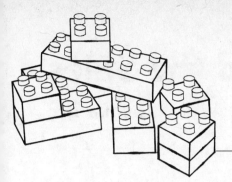

Ask Building Questions

- ○ I wonder if you have ever become really angry?
- ○ I wonder if you have ever done something you don't think God would like?
- ○ I wonder if it is hard to trust God?
- ○ I wonder if you have ever really messed something up?
- ○ I wonder if you have ever been so angry that you broke something very special?
- ○ I wonder how you felt once the special thing was broken?
- ○ I wonder what you do to get people's attention?
- ○ I wonder how others know you are angry?
- ○ I wonder if anyone has ever given you a second chance?
- ○ I wonder if anyone has ever helped you start over?

Suggest Blueprints (if needed)

- ○ two tablets with Ten Commandments
- ○ God
- ○ Moses
- ○ Aaron
- ○ Mount Horeb
- ○ Ark of the Covenant
- ○ Israelites
- ○ golden calf

Share Responses to the Story

Encourage each group member to share the creations they have made in response to the story. More details about sharing can be found on page 17.

Share a Snack

- ○ rice cereal treat "mountains"
- ○ cookie "tabernacles"
- ○ large cookie "tablets," decorated or plain

Continue the Story

One way to deepen the learning experience and create a link between group learning and faith formation in the home is to have builders show their creations to the adults who pick them up after class.

For additional study and conversation at home, consider different ways to share the Bible verses as well as some of the *Building Questions*. Possible methods of communication are texts, social media, e-blasts, website posts, and take-home sheets.

Rahab and the Spies
Joshua 1–2

Welcome the Group
Lay the Foundation
○ *Where is this story found in the Bible?*
Old Testament
○ *What is its place in the Bible story?*
after God chose Joshua to lead after Moses' death; before the Israelites crossed the Jordan River
○ *Who is the author?*
Joshua

○ *Who are the main characters?*
Joshua, Rahab, the spies, and God
○ *Where in the biblical world did it happen?*
Jericho
○ *Where is this in today's world?*
Jericho, near the Jordan River in the West Bank

Find the full description of *Lay the Foundation* on page 15.

Did You Know?
✔ Rahab was King David's great grandmother.
✔ Rahab was also in the same family line as Jesus.
✔ Both men and women were prostitutes in ancient times.
✔ Prostitution in Israel during Biblical setting was common, even thought it was against the law.

Pray
God, we thank you that everyone has an important place in your kingdom. Help us to reach out to one another in help and support. Make us people willing to serve you and by serving other. Amen.

Suggested prayer methods are outlined on page 15.

Share the Story
Suggestions for storytelling are detailed on page 16.

Note: Because Rahab was a prostitute, many storytellers may be tempted to skip over her story. I encourage you not to whitewash this story. We often get anxious and place a modern ethical overlay onto the fact that Rahab was a prostitute. It was fairly common during ancient times. People had fewer options for economic prosperity than they do now.

Rahab wasn't a shameful citizen of Jericho; she was a well-connected and well-known member of the community. Rahab ended up converting to Judaism following her rescue.

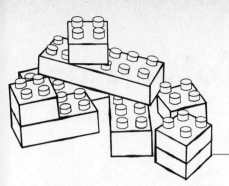

Respond to the Story

Invite each member of the group to use bricks and figures to respond to the story. This can be done individually or in small groups. Suggestions for how to support this form of theological reflection can be found on page 16.

Ask Building Questions

- ○ I wonder what it would feel like to be a leader of a whole nation?
- ○ I wonder if God has ever called you to be a leader?
- ○ I wonder if anyone close to you has ever died?
- ○ I wonder if you have ever experienced war?
- ○ I wonder if you have ever had to hide?
- ○ I wonder if lies can ever be helpful?
- ○ I wonder if anyone has needed your help?
- ○ I wonder if you have ever used a special sign or code word?
- ○ I wonder if you have made a promise to God?

Suggest Blueprints *(if needed)*

- ○ red cord
- ○ Rahab
- ○ Rahab's house
- ○ invasion
- ○ Jericho
- ○ spies
- ○ hiding place

Share Responses to the Story

Encourage each group member to share the creations they have made in response to the story. More details about sharing can be found on page 17.

Share a Snack

- ○ "red cord" shoestring licorice
- ○ shredded wheat "flax" stacks

Continue the Story

One way to deepen the learning experience and create a link between group learning and faith formation in the home is to have builders show their creations to the adults who pick them up after class.

For additional study and conversation at home, consider different ways to share the Bible verses as well as some of the *Building Questions*. Possible methods of communication are texts, social media, e-blasts, website posts, and take-home sheets.

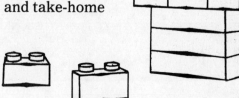

The Walls of Jericho
Joshua 6

Welcome the Group
Lay the Foundation

○ *Where is this story found in the Bible?*
Old Testament
○ *What is its place in the Bible story?*
after Rahab and the spies; before Joshua renewed his covenant with God
○ *Who is the author?*
Joshua

○ *Who are the main characters?*
Joshua, Rahab's family, priests, Israelite soldiers, Canaanite people and God
○ *Where in the biblical world did it happen?*
Jericho
○ *Where is this in today's world?*
Jericho, near the Jordan River in the West Bank

Find the full description of *Lay the Foundation* on page 15.

Did You Know?

✔ This story took place 40 years after the parting of the Red Sea.

✔ In the 1930s, archeologists found what they believe to be the remains of the walls of Jericho.

Pray

Dear God, break down the walls that separate us. Call us into a life together that is filled with love, mercy and truth. Heal the broken places in us so that we can live a life of joy and courage. Amen.

Suggested prayer methods are outlined on page 15.

Share the Story

Suggestions for storytelling are detailed on page 16.

Respond to the Story

Invite each member of the group to use bricks and figures to respond to the story. This can be done individually or in small groups. Suggestions for how to support this form of theological reflection can be found on page 16.

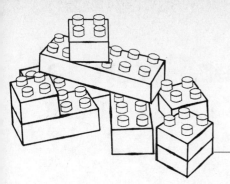

Ask Building Questions

○ I wonder if you have had to do something over and over?
○ I wonder if you have ever been close to war?
○ I wonder why wars happen?
○ I wonder if you have ever been close to a tall wall?
○ I wonder if you have ever wanted to enter somewhere but someone stopped you?
○ I wonder if you have ever marched?
○ I wonder if you have ever known a soldier?
○ I wonder if you have ever made a lot of noise?
○ I wonder if you have ever knocked anything down?
○ I wonder if you have ever been a part of a miracle?
○ I wonder if you have ever been to a place that has been destroyed?
○ I wonder if you make promises?
○ I wonder if you keep those promises?

Suggest Blueprints *(if needed)*

○ walls of Jericho
○ walls of Jericho destroyed
○ priests
○ soldiers
○ war
○ Joshua
○ ram's horns
○ God
○ Rahab and her family

Share Responses to the Story

Encourage each group member to share the creations they have made in response to the story. More details about sharing can be found on page 17.

Share a Snack

○ pudding cups stacked up like a wall
○ applesauce cups stacked up like a wall
○ pretzel nugget "stones"
○ "ram's horn" shaped snacks (Bugles®)

Continue the Story

One way to deepen the learning experience and create a link between group learning and faith formation in the home is to have builders show their creations to the adults who pick them up after class.

For additional study and conversation at home, consider different ways to share the Bible verses as well as some of the *Building Questions*. Possible methods of communication are texts, social media, e-blasts, website posts, and take-home sheets.

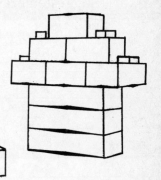

Hannah and Her Promise
1 Samuel 1:1–2:10

Welcome the Group
Lay the Foundation

○ *Where is this story found in the Bible?*
Old Testament
○ *What is its place in the Bible story?*
after Ruth married Boaz; before the Ark of the Covenant was captured
○ *Who is the author?*
at least four unknown sources

○ *Who are the main characters?*
Hannah, Eli, Samuel, and God
○ *Where in the biblical world did it happen?*
Shiloh
○ *Where is this in today's world?*
Er-Ram, north of Israel

Find the full description of *Lay the Foundation* on page 15.

Did You Know?

✔ Samuel was both a judge and a prophet.

✔ The name *Samuel* means "the name of God."

✔ Scholars believe that Samuel was 12 years old when God called him.

Pray

Dear God, help us to pray. Life can get so busy, so help us to remember that talking with you in prayer is a good place to be each day. Thank you God, for knowing us and loving us. Amen.

Suggested prayer methods are outlined on page 15.

Share the Story

Suggestions for storytelling are detailed on page 16.

Respond to the Story

Invite each member of the group to use bricks and figures to respond to the story. This can be done individually or in small groups. Suggestions for how to support this form of theological reflection can be found on page 16.

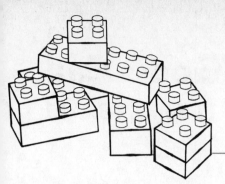

Ask Building Questions

- ○ I wonder if you have ever waited a long time for something?
- ○ I wonder what your prayers sound like?
- ○ I wonder if you have ever made a promise to God?
- ○ I wonder if God has ever made a promise to you?
- ○ I wonder if you have ever felt like God has forgotten about you?
- ○ I wonder if you have ever felt misunderstood?
- ○ I wonder if there is a story behind your name?
- ○ I wonder what it would be like to give your child away?
- ○ I wonder what you might do to be a part of God's story?

Suggest Blueprints *(if needed)*

- ○ baby Samuel
- ○ Hannah
- ○ temple
- ○ God

Share Responses to the Story

Encourage each group member to share the creations they have made in response to the story. More details about sharing can be found on page 17.

Share a Snack

- ○ graham-cracker "temples"
- ○ grape juice
- ○ matzo or pita bread
- ○ hummus

Continue the Story

One way to deepen the learning experience and create a link between group learning and faith formation in the home is to have builders show their creations to the adults who pick them up after class.

For additional study and conversation at home, consider different ways to share the Bible verses as well as some of the *Building Questions*. Possible methods of communication are texts, social media, e-blasts, website posts, and take-home sheets.

Samuel, Eli and God's Call
1 Samuel 3:1–4:1

Welcome the Group
Lay the Foundation

○ *Where is this story found in the Bible?*
Old Testament

○ *What is its place in the Bible story?*
after Hannah's prayer was answered; before the Ark of the Covenant was captured

○ *Who is the author?*
at least four unknown sources

○ *Who are the main characters?*
Eli, Samuel, and God

○ *Where in the biblical world did it happen?*
Shiloh

○ *Where is this in today's world?*
West Bank

Find the full description of *Lay the Foundation* on page 15.

Did You Know?

✔ Samuel was both a judge and a prophet.

✔ Historians, like Josephus, believe that Samuel was about 12 years old when he was called by God.

✔ Samuel was a helper to Eli, a priest. Normally this was a done by a son of the priest, but according to Scripture accounts, Eli's sons were wicked.

✔ Shiloh was the capital of Israel for hundreds of years before it was moved to Jerusalem.

Pray

Oh God, help us to listen for your voice calling to us. Make us ready to listen and serve. Amen.

Suggested prayer methods are outlined on page 15.

Share the Story

Suggestions for storytelling are detailed on page 16.

Respond to the Story

Invite each member of the group to use bricks and figures to respond to the story. This can be done individually or in small groups. Suggestions for how to support this form of theological reflection can be found on page 16.

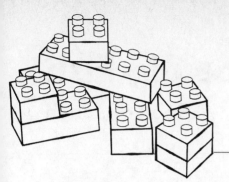

Ask Building Questions

○ I wonder if God has ever called your name?
○ I wonder if you know anyone who is blind?
○ I wonder if you know someone who is wise?
○ I wonder if you have ever met anyone wicked?
○ I wonder how we can help God?
○ I wonder what God might be saying to you?
○ I wonder what your special job might be?
○ I wonder if anyone has ever told you something that made your ears tingle?
○ I wonder what "sacrifice" means to you?
○ I wonder if you have ever met a prophet?

Suggest Blueprints *(if needed)*

○ Eli
○ Samuel
○ wicked brothers
○ temple
○ God
○ the people of Israel

Share Responses to the Story

Encourage each group member to share the creations they have made in response to the story. More details about sharing can be found on page 17.

Share a Snack

○ graham-cracker "temples"
○ grape juice
○ matzo or pita bread
○ hummus

Continue the Story

One way to deepen the learning experience and create a link between group learning and faith formation in the home is to have builders show their creations to the adults who pick them up after class.

For additional study and conversation at home, consider different ways to share the Bible verses as well as some of the *Building Questions*. Possible methods of communication are texts, social media, e-blasts, website posts, or take-home sheets.

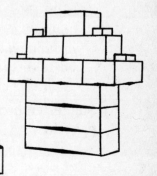

Jonah and the Big Fish
Book of Jonah

Welcome the Group
Lay the Foundation

○ *Where is this story found in the Bible?*
Old Testament

○ *What is its place in the Bible story?*
after the visions of the Prophet Obadiah; before the prophet Micah's messages of hope and salvation

○ *Who is the author?*
Jonah

○ *Who are the main characters?*
Jonah, sailors, people of Nineveh, and God

○ *Where in the biblical world did it happen?*
Ninevah

○ *Where is this in today's world?*
Northern Iraq

Find the full description of *Lay the Foundation* on page 15.

Did You Know?

✔ A prophet is someone who listens to the word of God and then tells others about God's message.

✔ The story of Jonah is also included in the Qur'an.

✔ Casting lots was a way of randomly making a decision or choosing a winner. The process is similar to rolling dice, playing rock-paper-scissors, or drawing the "short" stick. People often used bones or rocks to cast lots.

✔ Jesus talked about Jonah in the New Testament.

✔ Jonah was in the belly of the fish and Jesus was in the tomb the same amount of time—three days.

✔ The Book of Jonah is the only Old Testament book written for a Gentile nation.

Pray

Dear God, we don't always know the right thing to do. Help us to have courage, wisdom, and patience. Turn us around when we need it and give us the voice to speak your message. Amen.

Suggested prayer methods are outlined on page 15.

Share the Story

Suggestions for storytelling are detailed on page 16.

Respond to the Story

Invite each member of the group to use bricks and figures to respond to the story. This can be done individually or in small

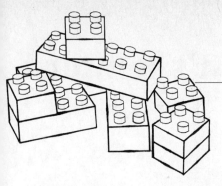

groups. Suggestions for how to support this form of theological reflection can be found on page 16.

Ask Building Questions

- ○ I wonder if you have ever heard the voice of God?
- ○ I wonder if God is trying to say something to us right now? to you?
- ○ I wonder if you have ever been close to a big body of water?
- ○ I wonder if you have ever been on a boat?
- ○ I wonder if you have ever been caught in a storm?
- ○ I wonder what it would feel like to run away from God?
- ○ I wonder if you have ever felt really confused?
- ○ I wonder if you have ever done something even though you were very afraid?
- ○ I wonder what it was like in the belly of the fish?
- ○ I wonder if you pray when you are afraid?
- ○ I wonder what it feels like to be the person who tells hard news?
- ○ I wonder if you have ever been given a second chance to do something?
- ○ I wonder if you have ever felt angry with God?

- ○ I wonder if you have ever felt protected by God?
- ○ I wonder how you tell others you are sorry?
- ○ I wonder why God does things that we don't understand?
- ○ I wonder what important things you have to say to the world?

Suggest Blueprints (if needed)

- ○ Jonah
- ○ God
- ○ fish
- ○ ocean
- ○ boat
- ○ sailors
- ○ people of Nineveh
- ○ king
- ○ animals
- ○ bush

Share Responses to the Story

Encourage each group member to share the creations they have made in response to the story. More details about sharing can be found on page 17.

Snack Ideas

- ○ blue gelatin
- ○ fish crackers
- ○ fish candies
- ○ white grape or apple juice tinted blue
- ○ thin pretzel sticks to be constructed into boats
- ○ broccoli "trees"

Continue the Story

One way to deepen the learning experience and create a link between group learning and faith formation in the home is to have builders show their creations to the adults who pick them up after class.

For additional study and conversation at home, consider different ways to share the Bible verses as well as some of the *Building Questions*. Possible methods of communication are texts, social media, e-blasts, website posts, and take-home sheets.

Solomon's Temple

1 Kings 6:1–8:66

Welcome the Group

Lay the Foundation

○ *Where is this story found in the Bible?*
Old Testament

○ *What is its place in the Bible story?*
after the death of King David; before the Queen of Sheba visited King Solomon

○ *Who is the author?*
unknown

○ *Who are the main characters?*
King Solomon, King Hiram, Priests, Israelites, and God

○ *Where in the biblical world did it happen?*
Temple Mount, Jerusalem

○ *Where is this in today's world?*
Mount Moriah, Jerusalem

Find the full description of *Lay the Foundation* on page 15.

Did You Know?

✔ King Solomon was King David's son.

✔ When this temple was finally built, it was the first permanent home for the Ark of the Covenant. Until then, the Ten Commandments were housed in a tent.

✔ King Solomon, known widely for his wisdom, is considered one of the major prophets in the Qur'an.

✔ King Solomon was the last king to rule over a united kingdom before it broke into two parts—the Kingdom of Israel and the Kingdom of Judah.

✔ Temple construction began 480 years after Pharaoh let the Israelites leave slavery in Egypt.

✔ According to Scripture, it took seven years to build the temple.

✔ The temple was built in the same place Abraham bound Isaac.

Pray

God of all places and all times, we thank you for coming to be with us. While we make homes for you on this earth, we know that you are at home everywhere. May all that we do and say be good, honest, and right. Amen.

Suggested prayer methods are outlined on page 15.

Share the Story

Suggestions for storytelling are detailed on page 16.

Note: This is another long passage with construction details and a step-by-step outline of how the temple was built and blessed. Consider studying this section and sharing the overarching themes and highlights instead of reading it word for word.

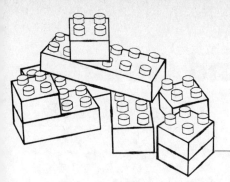

Respond to the Story

Invite each member of the group to use bricks and figures to respond to the story. This can be done individually or in small groups. Suggestions for how to support this form of theological reflection can be found on page 16.

Ask Building Questions

- ○ I wonder what you would build to honor God?
- ○ I wonder what is the biggest thing you have ever built?
- ○ I wonder if God has ever made a promise to you?
- ○ I wonder if you have ever been in a holy place?
- ○ I wonder if anyone has ever blessed you?
- ○ I wonder if you have blessed anyone?
- ○ I wonder why people build buildings for God?
- ○ I wonder if you have ever been inside a brand new church?
- ○ I wonder if God can be inside a building?
- ○ I wonder if you have been to a big party?
- ○ I wonder why people sacrificed animals to show their love for God?

Suggest Blueprints *(if needed)*

- ○ King Solomon
- ○ King Hiram
- ○ priests
- ○ people of Israel
- ○ temple building (parts or whole)
- ○ temple furnishings
- ○ animals for sacrifice
- ○ workers
- ○ Ark of the Covenant
- ○ celebration

Share Responses to the Story

Encourage each group member to share the creations they have made in response to the story. More details about sharing can be found on page 17.

Share a Snack

- ○ party foods
- ○ bread
- ○ grape juice
- ○ snack cups (fruit, pudding, applesauce, yogurt) stacked up to form a temple

Continue the Story

One way to deepen the learning experience and create a link between group learning and faith formation in the home is to have builders show their creations to the adults who pick them up after class.

For additional study and conversation at home, consider different ways to share the Bible verses as well as some of the *Building Questions*. Possible methods of communication are texts, social media, e-blasts, website posts, or take-home sheets.

David and Goliath
1 Samuel 17:1-58

Welcome the Group
Lay the Foundation

○ *Where is this story found in the Bible?*
Old Testament

○ *What is its place in the Bible story?*
after Samuel anointed David as the next king; before David and Jonathan became friends

○ *Who is the author?*
unknown

○ *Who are the main characters?*
David, Goliath, Philistine army, Israelites army, King Saul, David's Brothers, and God

○ *Where in the biblical world did it happen?*
Sokoh, Judah

○ *Where is this in today's world?*
Valley of Elah, near the West Bank

Find the full description of *Lay the Foundation* on page 15.

Did you know?

✔ The Bible describes Goliath as being six cubits high. By modern measurements that would make him 9' tall. A cubit is roughly 18" long. It was measured in ancient times by the length of one's arm from finger tip to top of the forearm.

✔ David and Goliath fought to decide who would be able to live in the land promised by God.

✔ Battles were fought by sending out the best soldier from each army.

Pray

God of power and mercy, thank you for your care and protection. Make us strong in your love and mighty in your will. Help us to remember that everyone can do something wonderful in your name. Amen.

Suggested prayer methods are outlined on page 15.

Share the Story

Suggestions for storytelling are detailed on page 16.

Respond to the Story

Invite each member of the group to use bricks and figures to respond to the story. This can be done individually or in small groups. Suggestions for how to support this form of theological reflection can be found on page 16.

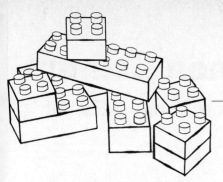

Ask Building Questions

- ○ I wonder why there were other people living in the land promised to the Israelites?
- ○ I wonder what made God choose David to be the leader?
- ○ I wonder if you have ever felt afraid of someone different than you?
- ○ I wonder if you have ever been a leader?
- ○ I wonder if you have been so angry with someone that you wanted to fight?
- ○ I wonder what Goliath sounded like when he spoke?
- ○ I wonder if the Philistines were afraid of him too?
- ○ I wonder if you can think of a time when you had to be very brave?
- ○ I wonder if anyone has ever thought you were too small or too young to do something?
- ○ I wonder if you have ever known for certain that God would protect you?
- ○ I wonder if there is ever a good reason to fight?
- ○ I wonder what important things you could do for God?

Suggest Blueprints *(if needed)*

- ○ David
- ○ Goliath
- ○ Philistine army
- ○ Israelite army
- ○ Saul
- ○ armor
- ○ David's brothers
- ○ Jesse
- ○ flock of sheep
- ○ slingshot and rock

Share Responses to the Story

Encourage each group member to share the creations they have made in response to the story. More details about sharing can be found on page 17.

Share a Snack

- ○ popcorn "rocks"
- ○ beef jerky
- ○ cheese
- ○ loaves of bread
- ○ marshmallow "sheep"
- ○ pretzel sticks

Continue the Story

One way to deepen the learning experience and create a link between group learning and faith formation in the home is to have builders show their creations to the adults who pick them up after class.

For additional study and conversation at home, consider different ways to share the Bible verses as well as some of the *Building Questions*. Possible methods of communication are texts, social media, e-blasts, website posts, or take-home sheets.

David and Goliath

Queen Esther
The Book of Esther

Welcome the Group
Lay the Foundation

○ *Where is this story found in the Bible?*
Old Testament

○ *What is its place in the Bible story?*
after the teachings of the prophet Nehemiah; before the story of Job

○ *Who is the author?*
unknown

○ *Who are the main characters?*
Esther, Haman, Mordecai, King Xerxes, Queen Vashti, and God

○ *Where in the biblical world did it happen?*
Susa, Upper Nile

○ *Where is this in today's world?*
Iran

Find the full description of *Lay the Foundation* on page 15.

Did You Know?

✔ The story of Esther is the basis for the Jewish festival of Purim.

✔ Esther's name comes from the Persian root for "morning star."

✔ Esther was an orphan.

✔ Esther was originally named *Hadassah*, meaning "myrtle." The myrtle tree is a symbol of the Jewish nation.

Pray

Dear God, give us wisdom and strength to do justice in the world. Give us bravery to act with courage to help others. Make us people who are willing to do what is right. Amen.

Suggested prayer methods are outlined on page 15.

Share the Story

Suggestions for storytelling are detailed on page 16.

Note: The story of Esther is full of gender role references. Again, we are tempted, as modern Christians, to place an overlay of our own current value system over stories like this one. I encourage you to focus your attention on the more positive and strong characteristics exhibited by Esther. She was an intelligent, generous, and direct woman who was able to do important and life-changing things for a whole nation of people. Esther has a lot to say to both our girls and boys about leadership and commitment to something bigger than one's self.

Respond to the Story

Invite each member of the group to use bricks and figures to respond to the story. This can be done individually or in small groups. Suggestions for how to support this form of theological reflection can be found on page 16.

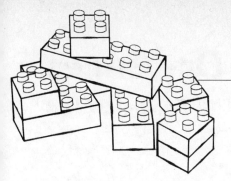

Ask Building Questions

○ I wonder what it is like to be a king?

○ I wonder if you have ever been to a very fancy party?

○ I wonder what it would be like to go to a celebration that lasts 180 days?

○ I wonder what it is like to do whatever you want?

○ I wonder if you think your "inside" or your "outside" parts are more important?

○ I wonder what it feels like to have to follow the commands of a king?

○ I wonder if you have ever felt like you needed to pretend to be something/someone different?

○ I wonder what it would be like to be far away from home?

○ I wonder if you have kept a secret about yourself?

○ I wonder if you have ever refused to go along with the crowd because you thought they were doing something wrong?

○ I wonder if you have ever thought a law was wrong?

○ I wonder if you have ever felt hated?

○ I wonder if you think money or people are more important?

○ I wonder if you have ever saved someone?

○ I wonder if you have ever had an enemy?

○ I wonder if you have ever had a hard time falling asleep?

○ I wonder if you have ever had an enemy?

○ I wonder if you have been someone's enemy?

○ I wonder what mercy means to you?

○ I wonder if you have special celebrations in your family?

Suggest Blueprints (if needed)

○ Queen Vashti

○ Persia

○ King Xerxes

○ Mordecai

○ Queen Esther

○ palace

○ crowns and royal clothing

○ king's officials and officers

○ Purim celebrations

○ Haman

○ King's gate

○ gallows

○ horses

○ battles

Share Responses to the Story

Encourage each group member to share the creations they have made in response to the story. More details about sharing can be found on page 17.

Share a Snack

○ Hamantaschen are the triangle cookies traditionally served at the festival of Purim. They can be filled with jelly. The name means "haman's pockets" or "Haman's ears."

○ grape juice

Continue the Story

One way to deepen the learning experience and create a link between group learning and faith formation in the home is to have builders show their creations to the adults who pick them up after class.

For additional study and conversation at home, consider different ways to share the Bible verses as well as some of the *Building Questions*. Possible methods of communication are texts, social media, e-blasts, website posts, or take-home sheets.

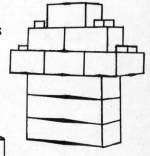

Valley of the Dry Bones
Ezekiel 37:1-14

Welcome the Group
Lay the Foundation

○ *Where is this story found in the Bible?*
Old Testament

○ *What is its place in the Bible story?*
after the prophecy to the mountains of Israel; before the prophecy of a new temple area

○ *Who is the author?*
the prophet Ezekiel

○ *Who are the main characters?*
Ezekiel, Israelites, and God

○ *Where in the biblical world did it happen?*
a vision of Ezekiel's, not an actual place

○ *Where is this in today's world?*
a vision of Ezekiel's, not an actual place

Find the full description of *Lay the Foundation* on page 15.

Did You Know?

✔ Ezekiel was a Hebrew prophet.

✔ A prophet is someone who listens to the word of God and then tells others about God's message

✔ Ezekiel's name means "may God strengthen him"

✔ Ezekiel is considered a prophet in Christian, Jewish, and Islamic traditions.

✔ The Valley of the Dry Bones was a vision seen by Ezekiel, not an actual place. He was referring to the rebirth of Israel.

Pray

Creator God, breathe into us the breath of your life and spirit. Fill us with hope and love. Let us always know you are with us and show us our home in you. Amen.

Suggested prayer methods are outlined on page 15.

Share the Story

Suggestions for storytelling are detailed on page 16.

Respond to the Story

Invite each member of the group to use bricks and figures to respond to the story. This can be done individually or in small groups. Suggestions for how to support this form of theological reflection can be found on page 16.

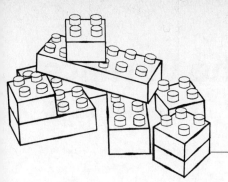

Ask Building Questions

- ❍ I wonder if you have ever heard God speak to you?
- ❍ I wonder what the word *prophet* means to you?
- ❍ I wonder if you have looked at a skeleton?
- ❍ I wonder if you have ever been close to a miracle when it happened?
- ❍ I wonder if there is anything that God can't do?
- ❍ I wonder if God has ever breathed on you?
- ❍ I wonder if you have ever been told a story you didn't understand?
- ❍ I wonder if you have ever felt the Holy Spirit?
- ❍ I wonder if you have ever felt taken care of by God?

Suggest Blueprints *(if needed)*

- ❍ skeletons
- ❍ whole bodies
- ❍ holy wind
- ❍ graves
- ❍ valley
- ❍ God
- ❍ Ezekiel
- ❍ Israelites

Share Responses to the Story

Encourage each group member to share the creations they have made in response to the story. More details about sharing can be found on page 17.

Share a Snack

- ❍ marshmallow-and-toothpick "skeletons"
- ❍ crumbled-cookie "deserts"
- ❍ graham-cracker "graves"

Continue the Story

One way to deepen the learning experience and create a link between group learning and faith formation in the home is to have builders show their creations to the adults who pick them up after class.

For additional study and conversation at home, consider different ways to share the Bible verses as well as some of the *Building Questions*. Possible methods of communication are texts, social media, e-blasts, website posts, or take-home sheets.

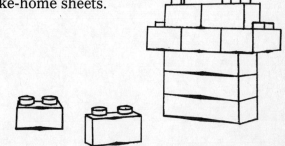

Fire in the Furnace
Daniel 3:1-30

Welcome the Group

Lay the Foundation

○ *Where is this story found in the Bible?*
Old Testament

○ *What is its place in the Bible story?*
after Daniel was made an advisor to King Nebuchadnezzar; before Daniel's visions

○ *Who is the author?*
unknown

○ *Who are the main characters?*
Shadrach, Meshach, Abednego, King Nebuchadnezzar, Daniel, the people of Babylon, and God

○ *Where in the biblical world did it happen?*
Babylon

○ *Where is this in today's world?*
Iraq

Find the full description of *Lay the Foundation* on page 15.

Did You Know?

✔ Daniel was a prophet who was speaking a message of encouragement for the Jewish people living in exile in Babylon.

✔ "Exile" means to be forced to stay away from the place you consider home.

✔ A prophet is someone who listens to the word of God and then tells others about God's message

✔ Daniel's name means "God is my judge" in Hebrew.

✔ Daniel is considered to be a prophet in the Jewish, Christian, and Islamic traditions.

Pray

Dear God, it is hard to stand up for what is right. Help us to know you are with us always, no matter what happens. Amen.

Suggested prayer methods are outlined on page 15.

Share the Story

Suggestions for storytelling are detailed on page 16.

Respond to the Story

Invite each member of the group to use bricks and figures to respond to the story. This can be done individually or in small groups. Suggestions for how to support this form of theological reflection can be found on page 16.

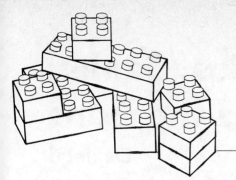

Ask Building Questions

- ❍ I wonder if you have ever felt that something or someone was more important than God?
- ❍ I wonder if you have ever done something because everyone else was doing it?
- ❍ I wonder if you have ever wanted to be different from those around you?
- ❍ I wonder if there are rules you don't want to follow?
- ❍ I wonder if anyone has ever tried to scare you into doing something you didn't want to do?
- ❍ I wonder if you have ever been close to a large fire?
- ❍ I wonder if someone has ever told you that God isn't important?
- ❍ I wonder if believing in God has ever felt dangerous?
- ❍ I wonder if you have ever been part of a miracle?
- ❍ I wonder if God has ever come very close to you?
- ❍ I wonder how you could help people believe that God is real?

Suggest Blueprints *(if needed)*

- ❍ King Nebuchadnezzar
- ❍ golden statue
- ❍ furnace
- ❍ Shadrach
- ❍ Meshach
- ❍ Abednego
- ❍ Babylon
- ❍ God
- ❍ musical instruments
- ❍ army guards
- ❍ fire
- ❍ angel

Share Responses to the Story

Encourage each group member to share the creations they have made in response to the story. More details about sharing can be found on page 17.

Share a Snack

- ❍ red, orange, and yellow gelatin "flames"
- ❍ spicy potato chips
- ❍ golden chocolate coins

Continue the Story

One way to deepen the learning experience and create a link between group learning and faith formation in the home is to have builders show their creations to the adults who pick them up after class.

For additional study and conversation at home, consider different ways to share the Bible verses as well as some of the *Building Questions*. Possible methods of communication are texts, social media, e-blasts, website posts, or take-home sheets.

King Darius, Daniel, and the Lions

Daniel 6

Welcome the Group

Lay the Foundation

- ○ *Where is this story found in the Bible?*
  Old Testament
- ○ *What is its place in the Bible story?*
  after the fiery furnace; before Daniel's visions
- ○ *Who is the author?*
  unknown

- ○ *Who are the main characters?*
  Daniel, King Darius, Lions, the people living in Babylon, and God
- ○ *Where in the biblical world did it happen?*
  Babylon
- ○ *Where is this in today's world?*
  Iraq

Find the full description of *Lay the Foundation* on page 15.

Did You Know?

- ✔ Daniel was a prophet who was speaking a message of encouragement for the Jewish people living in exile in Babylon.
- ✔ "Exile" means to be forced to stay away from the place you consider home.
- ✔ A prophet is someone who listens to the word of God and then tells others about God's message.
- ✔ Daniel's name means "God is my judge" in Hebrew.
- ✔ Daniel is considered to be a prophet in the Christian, Jewish, and Islamic traditions.

Pray

Give us your power and truth, O God. Protect us from the dangers of this world and make us willing to learn more and more about you each day. Amen.

Suggested prayer methods are outlined on page 15.

Share the Story

Suggestions for storytelling are detailed on page 16.

Respond to the Story

Invite each member of the group to use bricks and figures to respond to the story. This can be done individually or in small groups. Suggestions for how to support this form of theological reflection can be found on page 16.

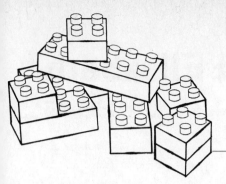

Ask Building Questions

○ I wonder if you have ever felt like you were the very best at something?

○ I wonder if you have ever been jealous of someone?

○ I wonder if you have ever known someone who tried to make bad or unfair rules?

○ I wonder if you have ever felt like you needed to keep your faith in God a secret?

○ I wonder if you have ever been tricked?

○ I wonder if believing in God has ever felt dangerous?

○ I wonder if you have ever made a bad choice?

○ I wonder if you have ever witnessed a miracle?

○ I wonder if you have felt the love and protection of God?

○ I wonder if you could help someone know more about God?

Suggest Blueprints *(if needed)*

○ King Darius

○ Daniel

○ Persian government officials

○ den

○ lions

○ God

Share Responses to the Story

Encourage each group member to share the creations they have made in response to the story. More details about sharing can be found on page 17.

Share a Snack

○ animal crackers

Note: You could omit the snack today to be like Daniel, who fasted in the lions den. It might be helpful to warn parents in advance if you plan to "fast" during class.

Continue the Story

One way to deepen the learning experience and create a link between group learning and faith formation in the home is to have builders show their creations to the adults who pick them up after class.

For additional study and conversation at home, consider different ways to share the Bible verses as well as some of the *Building Questions*. Possible methods of communication are texts, social media, e-blasts, website posts, or take-home sheets.

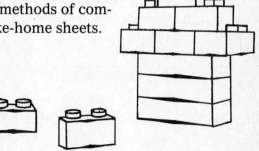

Mary and Elizabeth
Luke 1:39-45

Welcome the Group
Lay the Foundation

○ *Where is this story found in the Bible?*
New Testament

○ *What is its place in the Bible story?*
after the births of John the Baptist and Jesus were foretold; before the birth of Jesus

○ *Who is the author?*
Luke

○ *Who are the main characters?*
Elizabeth, Mary, Zechariah, Jesus (*still in Mary's womb*) **and John the Baptist** (*still in Elizabeth's womb*)

○ *Where in the biblical world did it happen?*
Hebron, hill country of Judea

○ *Where is this in today's world?*
Hebron, West Bank

Find the full description of *Lay the Foundation* on page 15.

Did You Know?

✔ Luke was commonly known as a doctor who traveled with Paul on his missionary trips.

✔ Luke never met Jesus.

✔ Luke is also the author of The Book of Acts.

✔ The book of Luke is a gospel book. A gospel is a recording of Jesus' life. There are four gospels in our Bible (Matthew, Mark, Luke, and John).

✔ Mary and Elizabeth were cousins, which made Jesus and John the Baptist cousins, too.

Pray

Dear God, create new places of joy and wonder in our lives. Help us to know the excitement of Jesus each day. Also, help us learn to wait for good things and trust in you. Amen.

Suggested prayer methods are outlined on page 15.

Share the Story

Suggestions for storytelling are detailed on page 16.

Note: If you are telling this story by heart, you may want to add details about the foretelling of the birth of John to Zechariah and the foretelling of the birth of Jesus to Mary and Joseph. These stories are interconnected; it would be helpful to lay the groundwork together.

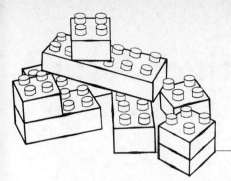

Respond to the Story

Invite each member of the group to use bricks and figures to respond to the story. This can be done individually or in small groups. Suggestions for how to support this form of theological reflection can be found on page 16.

Ask Building Questions

- ○ I wonder if you have ever felt the belly of someone who is pregnant?
- ○ I wonder if you have a cousin?
- ○ I wonder what you do when you are excited?
- ○ I wonder what song you would sing for God?
- ○ I wonder if you have ever been asked to do something important for God?
- ○ I wonder what you think "blessed" means?
- ○ I wonder if you have ever felt blessed?

Suggest Blueprints *(if needed)*

- ○ Mary
- ○ Elizabeth
- ○ hill country of Judea
- ○ Elizabeth and Zechariah's house
- ○ God

Share Responses to the Story

Encourage each group member to share the creations they have made in response to the story. More details about sharing can be found on page 17.

Share a Snack

- ○ cut vegetables or fruit
- ○ grape juice
- ○ pita bread

Continue the Story

One way to deepen the learning experience and create a link between group learning and faith formation in the home is to have builders show their creations to the adults who pick them up after class.

For additional study and conversation at home, consider different ways to share the Bible verses as well as some of the *Building Questions.* Possible methods of communication are texts, social media, e-blasts, website posts, or take-home sheets.

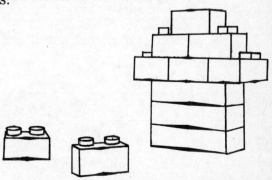

Mary and Elizabeth

The Birth of Jesus
Matthew 1:18-25; Luke 2:1-20

Welcome the Group

Lay the Foundation

○ *Where is this story found in the Bible?*
New Testament

○ *What is its place in the Bible story?*
after Mary and Joseph's journey to Bethlehem; before the flight into Egypt

○ *Who is the author?*
Matthew and Luke

○ *Who are the main characters?*
Jesus, Mary, Joseph, angels, shepherds, and God

○ *Where in the biblical world did it happen?*
Bethlehem

○ *Where is this in today's world?*
Bethlehem, West Bank

Find the full description of *Lay the Foundation* on page 15.

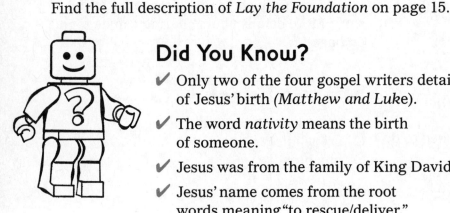

Did You Know?

✔ Only two of the four gospel writers detail the story of Jesus' birth (*Matthew and Luke*).

✔ The word *nativity* means the birth of someone.

✔ Jesus was from the family of King David.

✔ Jesus' name comes from the root words meaning "to rescue/deliver."

✔ Another name of Jesus is *Emmanuel*, which means "God is with us."

Pray

Dear God, come into our hearts with hope and joy. Let us always remember that Jesus is our greatest gift. Amen.

Suggested prayer methods are outlined on page 15.

Share the Story

Suggestions for storytelling are detailed on page 16.

Respond to the Story

Invite each member of the group to use bricks and figures to respond to the story. This can be done individually or in small groups. Suggestions for how to support this form of theological reflection can be found on page 16.

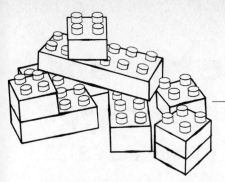

Ask Building Questions

- ○ I wonder what you know about the birth of Jesus?
- ○ I wonder if you have ever been close to a tiny baby?
- ○ I wonder why God chose to send Jesus as a baby instead of as an adult?
- ○ I wonder if you have more than one name?
- ○ I wonder if you have ever been counted in a census?
- ○ I wonder if you have ever been on a long trip?
- ○ I wonder if you have ever had a hard time finding a place to sleep?
- ○ I wonder what your parents thought about when you were born?
- ○ I wonder what God was thinking on the day you were born?
- ○ I wonder if you have ever seen an angel?
- ○ I wonder if God has ever told you good news?
- ○ I wonder what the shepherds thought when they met Jesus?
- ○ I wonder what the world would be like without Jesus?
- ○ I wonder if you have special ways to remember the birth of Jesus?
- ○ I wonder if you have witnessed a sign from God?

Suggest Blueprints *(if needed)*

- ○ Emperor Augustus
- ○ Mary
- ○ Joseph
- ○ Jesus
- ○ inn keepers
- ○ shepherds
- ○ angels
- ○ Bethlehem
- ○ stable
- ○ star
- ○ animals
- ○ God

Share Responses to the Story

Encourage each group member to share the creations they have made in response to the story. More details about sharing can be found on page 17.

Share a Snack

- ○ star cookies
- ○ angel cookies
- ○ for longer snack time, gingerbread "mangers" or "barns"

Continue the Story

One way to deepen the learning experience and create a link between group learning and faith formation in the home is to have builders show their creations to the adults who pick them up after class.

For additional study and conversation at home, consider different ways to share the Bible verses as well as some of the *Building Questions*. Possible methods of communication are texts, social media, e-blasts, website posts, or take-home sheets.

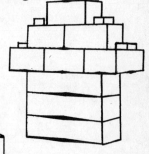

The Wise Men and the Escape to Egypt
Matthew 2:1-23

Welcome the Group
Lay the Foundation

○ *Where is this story found in the Bible?*
New Testament

○ *What is its place in the Bible story?*
after the birth of Jesus; before the return of Mary, Joseph, and Jesus from Egypt

○ *Who is the author?*
Matthew

○ *Who are the main characters?*
Mary, Joseph, wise men, Jesus, King Herod, angel, and God

○ *Where in the biblical world did it happen?*
Egypt

○ *Where is this in today's world?*
Egypt

Find the full description of *Lay the Foundation* on page 15.

Did You Know?

✔ Only one gospel writer (Matthew) includes the wise men in his writings.

✔ Matthew was an actual follower of Jesus and is sometimes called "Levi" in the Bible.

✔ The word *Magi* comes from the word for "magician" in several different languages. Magi (or wise men) were scholars who studied astrology (stars and other heavenly bodies), alchemy (chemistry), and other sciences.

✔ The Bible does not mention the number of wise men who visited Jesus and his family.

✔ The Wise Men are also sometimes called "kings."

✔ Their journey may have taken several years.

Pray

Dear God, make us people who search for your love and goodness. Let us follow the star to you and keep our eyes on you each day. Help us to remember that there is no greater gift than your son, Jesus. Amen.

Suggested prayer methods are outlined on page 15.

Share the Story

Suggestions for storytelling are detailed on page 16.

Respond to the Story

Invite each member of the group to use bricks and figures to respond to the story. This can be done individually or in small groups. Suggestions for how to support this form of theological reflection can be found on page 16.

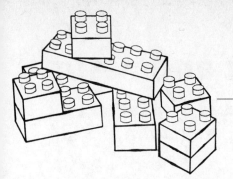

Ask Building Questions

○ I wonder if you have spent time looking up at the stars?

○ I wonder if you have ever seen a bright star in the night sky?

○ I wonder if anyone has come to visit you from far away?

○ I wonder why they called them *wise* men?

○ I wonder if there were any wise *women* on the journey too?

○ I wonder what you would bring to baby Jesus as your gift?

○ I wonder what "Messiah" means to you?

○ I wonder if you have ever been close to a frightened adult?

○ I wonder why the king was very afraid?

○ I wonder if anyone has wanted you to help him or her do a bad thing?

○ I wonder if you have had a vivid dream?

○ I wonder if you have ever felt like you were in danger?

○ I wonder if you believe in angels?

○ I wonder if you have ever been given a message from God?

○ I wonder who keeps you safe?

○ I wonder what it feels like to really trust in God?

Suggest Blueprints *(if needed)*

○ Mary
○ Joseph
○ Jesus
○ angel
○ King Herod
○ babies
○ Wise Men
○ God

Share Responses to the Story

Encourage each group member to share the creations they have made in response to the story. More details about sharing can be found on page 17.

Share a Snack

○ star-shaped cookies
○ star fruit or vegetable cutouts
○ crown cookies
○ crown fruit or vegetable cutouts

Continue the Story

One way to deepen the learning experience and create a link between group learning and faith formation in the home is to have builders show their creations to the adults who pick them up after class.

For additional study and conversation at home, consider different ways to share the Bible verses as well as some of the *Building Questions*. Possible methods of communication are texts, social media, e-blasts, website posts, or take-home sheets.

John the Baptist and Jesus

Matthew 3:13-17; Mark 1:1-11; Luke 3; John 1:19-34

Welcome the Group

Lay the Foundation

○ *Where is this story found in the Bible?*
New Testament
○ *What is its place in the Bible story?*
after Mary, Joseph, and Jesus returned from Egypt to Nazareth; before Jesus called his first disciples
○ *Who is the author?*
Matthew, Mark, Luke, and John all gave their own accounts

○ *Who are the main characters?*
John the Baptist, Jesus, Holy Spirit, and God
○ *Where in the biblical world did it happen?*
Jordan River
○ *Where is this in today's world?*
Jordan River

Find the full description of *Lay the Foundation* on page 15.

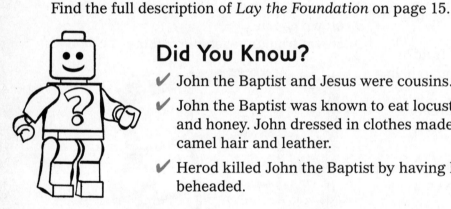

Did You Know?

✔ John the Baptist and Jesus were cousins.

✔ John the Baptist was known to eat locusts and honey. John dressed in clothes made of camel hair and leather.

✔ Herod killed John the Baptist by having him beheaded.

Pray

Dear God, thank for making us a part of your family. Through baptism, help us remember how you made us new and brought us to everlasting life. Amen.

Suggested prayer methods are outlined on page 15.

Share the Story

Suggestions for storytelling are detailed on page 16.

Respond to the Story

Invite each member of the group to use bricks and figures to respond to the story. This can be done individually or in small groups. Suggestions for how to support this form of theological reflection can be found on page 16.

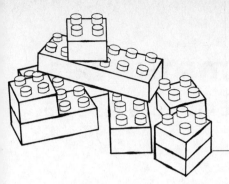

Ask Building Questions

- I wonder if anyone has told you a story from your baptism?
- I wonder what really happens when a person is baptized?
- I wonder what it means to be baptized with fire and the Holy Spirit?
- I wonder why John chose to live such a different life than everyone else?
- I wonder what the word *repent* means to you?
- I wonder what it feels like to meet someone different from you?
- I wonder if John the Baptist was ever jealous of Jesus?
- I wonder if you have ever had an important message to share?
- I wonder what it feels like to wait?
- I wonder why Jesus wanted to be baptized?
- I wonder what the Holy Spirit feels like? sounds like? smells like? looks like?
- I wonder what God said (will say) on the day of your baptism?
- I wonder if you realize you are a beloved child of God, too?

Suggest Blueprints (if needed)

- John
- Jesus
- God
- Holy Spirit as dove
- Holy Spirit as fire
- John's clothing (camel hair and leather)
- John's food (locusts and honey)
- baptism
- River Jordan
- parting skies
- Pharisees
- Sadducees

Share Responses to the Story

Encourage each group member to share the creations they have made in response to the story. More details about sharing can be found on page 17.

Share a Snack

- chocolate covered insects
- gummy insects
- insect-shaped cookies
- construct insects with marshmallows, jelly beans, and licorice strips
- honey dip with fruit or graham crackers
- beef jerky or dried meats
- water
- dove-shaped rice treats, cookies, fruit, or cheese
- watermelon "flame" cut outs

Continue the Story

One way to deepen the learning experience and create a link between group learning and faith formation in the home is to have builders show their creations to the adults who pick them up after class.

For additional study and conversation at home, consider different ways to share the Bible verses as well as some of the *Building Questions*. Possible methods of communication are texts, social media, e-blasts, website posts, or take-home sheets.

Jesus Calms the Sea
Matthew 8:23-27; Mark 4:35-41; Luke 8:22-25

Welcome the Group

Lay the Foundation

○ *Where is this story found in the Bible?*
New Testament

○ *What is its place in the Bible story?*
after Jesus' parables; before Jesus cast out a demon by sending it into a herd of pigs

○ *Who is the author?*
Matthew, Mark, and Luke

○ *Who are the main characters?*
Jesus, the disciples and God

○ *Where in the biblical world did it happen?*
Sea of Galilee

○ *Where is this in today's world?*
Sea of Galilee, near the Golan Heights of northeast Israel

Find the full description of *Lay the Foundation* on page 15.

Did You Know?

✔ The word *disciple* comes from the Latin word for "student" or "apprentice."

✔ The Sea of Galilee is 13 miles long and eight miles wide.

✔ The Sea of Galilee is also called Lake Gennesaret or Lake Tiberias.

Pray

Dear God, sometimes we experience rough seas. Life isn't always what we expect. Comfort us. Protect us. Love and hold us so we won't be afraid. Lift us up when we fall and walk with us all the days of our lives. Amen.

Suggested prayer methods are outlined on page 15.

Share the Story

Suggestions for storytelling are detailed on page 16.

Respond to the Story

Invite each member of the group to use bricks and figures to respond to the story. This can be done individually or in small groups. Suggestions for how to support this form of theological reflection can be found on page 16.

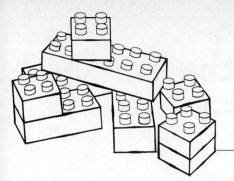

Ask Building Questions

- ○ I wonder if you have ever been on a boat?
- ○ I wonder if you have ever been close to a large body of water?
- ○ I wonder if you have ever been caught in a storm?
- ○ I wonder if you have ever been very afraid?
- ○ I wonder if you have asked God for help when you were afraid?
- ○ I wonder what the disciples thought when the storm was raging?
- ○ I wonder if you have ever felt like you didn't have faith in God?
- ○ I wonder if you know anyone who has a lot of faith in God?

Suggest Blueprints *(if needed)*

- ○ Boat
- ○ Jesus
- ○ disciples
- ○ water
- ○ storm
- ○ waves
- ○ calm waters
- ○ God

Share Responses to the Story

Encourage each group member to share the creations they have made in response to the story. More details about sharing can be found on page 17.

Share a Snack

- ○ blue gelatin blocks to make stormy waves and calm seas
- ○ pita-pocket "boats" with veggies or hummus

Continue the Story

One way to deepen the learning experience and create a link between group learning and faith formation in the home is to have builders show their creations to the adults who pick them up after class.

For additional study and conversation at home, consider different ways to share the Bible verses as well as some of the *Building Questions*. Possible methods of communication are texts, social media, e-blasts, website posts, or take-home sheets.

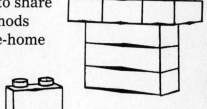

Feeding the Masses

Matthew 14:31-21; Mark 6:30-44; Luke 9:10-17; John 6:1-15

Welcome the Group

Lay the Foundation

○ *Where is this story found in the Bible?*
New Testament

○ *What is its place in the Bible story?*
after Jesus' healing miracles; before Jesus walked on water

○ *Who is the author?*
Matthew, Mark, Luke, and John

○ *Who are the main characters?*
Jesus, disciples, young boy, a crowd of people, and God

○ *Where in the biblical world did it happen?*
Sea of Galilee

○ *Where is this in today's world?*
Sea of Galilee, near the Golan Heights of Northeast Israel

Find the full description of *Lay the Foundation* on page 15.

Did You Know?

✔ The feeding of the masses is the only miracle detailed in all four gospels.

✔ There were far more than 5,000 people there. Five thousand only indicates the adult men in the group. There could have been as many as 20,000 people with women, children, and servants.

✔ Matthew and Mark tell two different accounts of feeding the masses.

Pray

Dear God, having faith can be hard sometimes. Help us to see that there is always enough when it comes to your love and care. Show us ways to help share with others, and increase joy and love in all God's people. Amen.

Suggested prayer methods are outlined on page 15.

Share the Story

Suggestions for storytelling are detailed on page 16.

Respond to the Story

Invite each member of the group to use bricks and figures to respond to the story. This can be done individually or in small groups. Suggestions for how to support this form of theological reflection can be found on page 16.

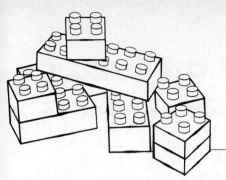

Ask Building Questions

○ I wonder if you have ever been hungry?
○ I wonder if you have ever had to go without eating?
○ I wonder if you have ever been a part of a very large crowd?
○ I wonder if you have ever been part of a miracle?
○ I wonder what Jesus could have been talking about for three whole days?
○ I wonder if you have ever wanted to be alone but you couldn't be?
○ I wonder what you like to do when you are alone?
○ I wonder if you have ever shared something with a lot of people, yet there was enough for everyone?
○ I wonder if it would be hard to share your food if you were really hungry?
○ I wonder what it felt like to be healed by Jesus?
○ I wonder what the Kingdom of God might be like?

Suggest Blueprints *(if needed)*

○ Jesus
○ disciples
○ crowd
○ fish and loaves of bread
○ leftover food
○ Sea of Galilee
○ boat
○ mountain

Share Responses to the Story

Encourage each group member to share the creations they have made in response to the story. More details about sharing can be found on page 17.

Share a Snack

○ loaves of bread to be torn apart by group
○ fish
○ candy or cookie fish
○ mini shredded wheat

Note: This might be the perfect day to eat picnic-style instead of at the table.

Continue the Story

One way to deepen the learning experience and create a link between group learning and faith formation in the home is to have builders show their creations to the adults who pick them up after class.

For additional study and conversation at home, consider different ways to share the Bible verses as well as some of the *Building Questions*. Possible methods of communication are texts, social media, e-blasts, website posts, or take-home sheets.

Feeding the Masses

Jesus Walks on Water
Matthew 14:22-36; Mark 6:45-56; John 6:16-24

Welcome the Group

Lay the Foundation

○ *Where is this story found in the Bible?*
New Testament

○ *What is its place in the Bible story?*
after feeding of the masses; before the healing stories

○ *Who is the author?*
Matthew, Mark, and John

○ *Who are the main characters?*
Jesus, disciples, and God

○ *Where in the biblical world did it happen?*
Sea of Galilee

○ *Where is this in today's world?*
Sea of Galilee

Find the full description of *Lay the Foundation* on page 15.

Did You Know?

✔ The Gospel of Matthew is the only gospel that mentions Peter walking out into the water to meet Jesus.

✔ The Sea of Galilee is 13 miles long and eight miles wide.

✔ The Sea of Galilee is also called Lake Gennesaret or Lake Tiberias.

✔ The name *Peter* refers to Peter being the "rock" *(Petra)* of the church. Many people recognize Peter as the first bishop of the church.

Pray

Lift us up, O God, and make us strong. Encourage us when we doubt, and help us up when we fall. Remind us that if we keep our eyes on you, we will know more peace. Amen.

Suggested prayer methods are outlined on page 15.

Share the Story

Suggestions for storytelling are detailed on page 16.

Respond to the Story

Invite each member of the group to use bricks and figures to respond to the story. This can be done individually or in small groups. Suggestions for how to support this form of theological reflection can be found on page 16.

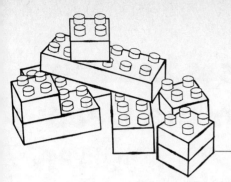

Ask Building Questions

- ○ I wonder where you go to pray? (or *could* go to pray?)
- ○ I wonder what you like to do when you are alone?
- ○ I wonder if you have ever been on rough seas?
- ○ I wonder if you have ever been close to a miracle?
- ○ I wonder if something has happened and you couldn't believe what you were seeing?
- ○ I wonder what it is like to follow Jesus?
- ○ I wonder what it felt like to step out of the boat and onto the water?
- ○ I wonder if you trust God?
- ○ I wonder if we can doubt and trust at the same time?
- ○ I wonder how you would like to worship God?

Suggest Blueprints *(if needed)*

- ○ boat
- ○ Jesus
- ○ disciples
- ○ Peter
- ○ water
- ○ rough waves
- ○ God

Share Responses to the Story

Encourage each group member to share the creations they have made in response to the story. More details about sharing can be found on page 17.

Share a Snack

- ○ blue gelatin blocks to make stormy waves and calm seas
- ○ pita-pocket "boats" with veggies or hummus

Continue the Story

One way to deepen the learning experience and create a link between group learning and faith formation in the home is to have builders show their creations to the adults who pick them up after class.

For additional study and conversation at home, consider different ways to share the Bible verses as well as some of the *Building Questions*. Possible methods of communication are texts, social media, e-blasts, website posts, or take-home sheets.

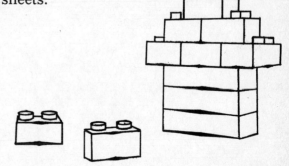

Jesus Raises Lazarus from the Dead

John 11:1-44

Welcome the Group

Lay the Foundation

○ *Where is this story found in the Bible?*
New Testament

○ *What is its place in the Bible story?*
after the parable of the Good Shepherd; before the plot to kill Jesus

○ *Who is the author?*
John

○ *Who are the main characters?*
Lazarus, Mary, Martha, Jesus, and God

○ *Where in the biblical world did it happen?*
Bethany

○ *Where is this in today's world?*
West Bank city of al-Eizariya

Find the full description of *Lay the Foundation* on page 15.

Did You Know?

✔ In the Jewish tradition, three days after the death is a time to "sit shiva." It is a time to light a candle and welcome mourners. The fact that Jesus arrived after that time was a dramatic sign that he truly had power over life and death. He truly was the "resurrection and the life."

Pray

Help us trust you, God, when things go wrong or we are afraid. Show us that you have power and you give life. We thank you for brothers and sisters and all the ways we know the love of family. Amen.

Suggested prayer methods are outlined on page 15.

Share the Story

Suggestions for storytelling are detailed on page 16.

Respond to the Story

Invite each member of the group to use bricks and figures to respond to the story. This can be done individually or in small groups. Suggestions for how to support this form of theological reflection can be found on page 16.

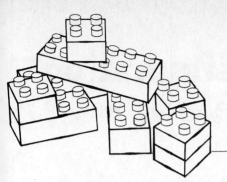

Ask Building Questions

○ I wonder if you have ever had a family member die?

○ I wonder if your family has special things they do to remember dead friends and family?

○ I wonder if Jesus has ever disappointed you?

○ I wonder what it was like to be a disciple of Jesus?

○ I wonder what it is like to completely trust in God?

○ I wonder what it will be like to live forever with God?

○ I wonder if the story of the tomb reminds you of any other stories?

Suggest Blueprints *(if needed)*

○ Martha
○ Mary
○ Lazarus
○ Jesus

○ God
○ crowd
○ tomb
○ bandages
○ death
○ life

Share Responses to the Story

Encourage each group member to share the creations they have made in response to the story. More details about sharing can be found on page 17.

Share a Snack

○ muffin "tombs" (top pulled off and insides slightly hollowed out)

○ cotton-candy "bands of cloth"

○ marshmallow-creme "bandages" on a cookie "person"

Continue the Story

One way to deepen the learning experience and create a link between group learning and faith formation in the home is to have builders show their creations to the adults who pick them up after class.

For additional study and conversation at home, consider different ways to share the Bible verses as well as some of the *Building Questions*. Possible methods of communication are texts, social media, e-blasts, website posts, or take-home sheets.

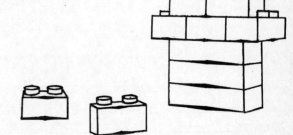

Jesus Raises Lazarus from the Dead

The Transfiguration
Matthew 17:1-9; Mark 9:2-13; Luke 9:28-36

Welcome the Group

Lay the Foundation

○ *Where is this story found in the Bible?*
New Testament

○ *What is its place in the Bible story?*
after Jesus foretold his death and resurrection; before Jesus cured a young boy who had a demon spirit

○ *Who is the author?*
Matthew, Mark, and Luke each have their own accounts

○ *Who are the main characters?*
Jesus, Peter, James, John, Elijah, Moses, and God

○ *Where in the biblical world did it happen?*
unknown

○ *Where is this in today's world?*
Mount Tabor, Israel, Lower Galilee

Find the full description of *Lay the Foundation* on page 15.

Did You Know?

✔ The word *transfiguration* means (in Biblical terms) to completely change your appearance or state into something more beautiful or holy.

Pray

Come into this place, O God. Let us feel your presence and know your love. Teach us about all the faithful people who have followed you since the beginning of time. Amen.

Suggested prayer methods are outlined on page 15.

Share the Story

Suggestions for storytelling are detailed on page 16.

Respond to the Story

Invite each member of the group to use bricks and figures to respond to the story. This can be done individually or in small groups. Suggestions for how to support this form of theological reflection can be found on page 16.

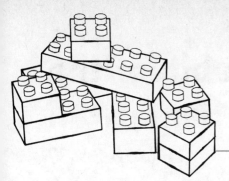

Ask Building Questions

- ○ I wonder who are your closest friends?
- ○ I wonder if you have ever felt something change within you?
- ○ I wonder what it was like for Peter, James, and John to be there when Jesus shone like the sun?
- ○ I wonder if you have ever seen a vision?
- ○ I wonder why Moses and Elijah appeared?
- ○ I wonder if you have ever wanted to stay in a special place forever?
- ○ I wonder if you have heard the voice of God?
- ○ I wonder what the voice of God might sound like?
- ○ I wonder if you have kept a secret for someone?
- ○ I wonder if you have ever been in a holy place?
- ○ I wonder if you know any holy people?
- ○ I wonder if you have ever felt holy?

Suggest Blueprints *(if needed)*

- ○ God in the cloud
- ○ Jesus transfigured
- ○ Peter
- ○ James
- ○ John
- ○ visions of Moses and Elijah
- ○ mountain

Share Responses to the Story

Encourage each group member to share the creations they have made in response to the story. More details about sharing can be found on page 17.

Share a Snack

- ○ mountain of cookies piled up to share

Continue the Story

One way to deepen the learning experience and create a link between group learning and faith formation in the home is to have builders show their creations to the adults who pick them up after class.

For additional study and conversation at home, consider different ways to share the Bible verses as well as some of the *Building Questions*. Possible methods of communication are texts, social media, e-blasts, website posts, or take-home sheets.

The Transfiguration

The Parable of the Good Samaritan

Luke 10:25-37

Welcome the Group

Lay the Foundation

○ *Where is this story found in the Bible?*
New Testament

○ *What is its place in the Bible story?*
after Jesus' transfiguration; before Jesus visited Martha and Mary

○ *Who is the author?*
Luke

○ *Who are the main characters?*
Jesus, lawyer, disciples, and God

○ *Where in the biblical world did it happen?*
a parable, not an actual location

○ *Where is this in today's world?*
a parable, not an actual location

Find the full description of *Lay the Foundation* on page 15.

Did You Know

✔ A parable is a simple story to explain an important lesson or point. Jesus used parables to explain many things, including heaven and the Kingdom of God on earth.

✔ Luke is the only gospel writer to include the parable of the Good Samaritan.

✔ This parable is a story told by Jesus, so the priest, Levite, and Samaritan and wounded man are all fictional.

✔ Why might the priest and Levite not stop to help? Because for them to touch a dead person made them ritually "unclean" and unable to serve in their roles for at least seven days.

Pray

Dear God, helper of all, teach us to help others in need. Show us that we are all in need of your help. Let us reach out to make the world better. Amen.

Suggested prayer methods are outlined on page 15.

Share the Story

Suggestions for storytelling are detailed on page 16.

Respond to the Story

Invite each member of the group to use bricks and figures to respond to the story. This can be done individually or in small groups. Suggestions for how to support this form of theological reflection can be found on page 16.

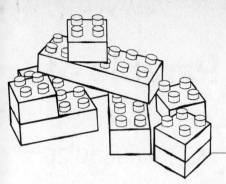

Ask Building Questions

- ○ I wonder why some people didn't believe that Jesus was the Son of God?
- ○ I wonder who is your "neighbor"?
- ○ I wonder if you have ever helped someone who was hurt?
- ○ I wonder if it is ever hard to do the right thing?
- ○ I wonder if you have ever wanted to help someone but were afraid to do it?
- ○ I wonder why some people pretend not to see people who need help?
- ○ I wonder if anyone has ever told you a story to help you understand something confusing?
- ○ I wonder who helps you when you need it?
- ○ I wonder in what ways we can help others?
- ○ I wonder where God might be in this story?
- ○ I wonder where you might be in this story?

Suggest Blueprints (if needed)

- ○ Jesus
- ○ Lawyer
- ○ wounded man
- ○ priest
- ○ Levite
- ○ Samaritan
- ○ horse
- ○ innkeeper
- ○ God

Share Responses

Encourage each group member to share the creations they have made in response to the story. More details about sharing can be found on page 17.

Share a Snack

- ○ foods typically consumed when one is sick: ginger ale, crackers, bottled water, cough drops, juice, rice cakes, gelatin, soup broth

Continue the Story

One way to deepen the learning experience and create a link between group learning and faith formation in the home is to have builders show their creations to the adults who pick them up after class.

For additional study and conversation at home, consider different ways to share the Bible verses as well as some of the *Building Questions*. Possible methods of communication are texts, social media, e-blasts, website posts, or take-home sheets.

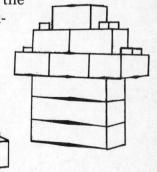

The Parable of the Good Samaritan

The Parable of the Lost Sheep

Matthew 18:10-14; Luke 15:1-7; John 10:26

Welcome the Group

Lay the Foundation

○ *Where is this story found in the Bible?*
New Testament

○ *What is its place in the Bible story?*
after Jesus foretold his death and resurrection; before Jesus preached about forgiveness

○ *Who is the author?*
Matthew, Luke, and John

○ *Who are the main characters?*
Jesus, disciples, tax collectors, sinners, Pharisees, scribes, good shepherd, sheep, and God

○ *Where in the biblical world did it happen?*
a parable, not an actual location

○ *Where is this in today's world?*
a parable, not an actual location

Find the full description of *Lay the Foundation* on page 15.

Did You Know?

✔ A parable is a simple story to explain an important lesson or point. Jesus used parables to explain many things including heaven and the Kingdom of God on earth.

Pray

Protector and lover of us all, thank you for showing us the way and leading us each day. Help us to listen to your voice and follow you. Keep us in safe places and remind us of your care. Amen.

Suggested prayer methods are outlined on page 15.

Share the Story

Suggestions for storytelling are detailed on page 16.

Respond to the Story

Invite each member of the group to use bricks and figures to respond to the story. This can be done individually or in small groups. Suggestions for how to support this form of theological reflection can be found on page 16.

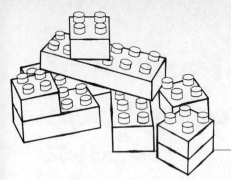

Ask Building Questions

- ○ I wonder what it is like to be a shepherd?
- ○ I wonder if you would like to be a shepherd?
- ○ I wonder what it is like to be a sheep?
- ○ I wonder how the shepherd can really know all the sheep in his/her flock?
- ○ I wonder if you have ever been lost?
- ○ I wonder if you have ever tried to get lost?
- ○ I wonder what it felt like to be found?
- ○ I wonder if you think God really knows you?
- ○ I wonder if you know God loves you?
- ○ I wonder what rejoicing with God feels like?
- ○ I wonder where God is in this story?
- ○ I wonder where you are in this story?

Suggest Blueprints *(if needed)*

- ○ Jesus
- ○ tax collectors and sinners
- ○ Pharisees and scribes
- ○ shepherd
- ○ flock for sheep
- ○ lost sheep
- ○ celebration

Share Responses to the Story

Encourage each group member to share the creations they have made in response to the story. More details about sharing can be found on page 17.

Share a Snack

- ○ marshmallow "sheep"
- ○ party food

Continue the Story

One way to deepen the learning experience and create a link between group learning and faith formation in the home is to have builders show their creations to the adults who pick them up after class.

For additional study and conversation at home, consider different ways to share the Bible verses as well as some of the *Building Questions*. Possible methods of communication are texts, social media, e-blasts, website posts, or take-home sheets.

The Parable of the Lost Sheep

The Parable of the Prodigal Son

Luke 15:11-32

Welcome the Group

Lay the Foundation

○ *Where is this story found in the Bible?*
New Testament

○ *What is its place in the Bible story?*
after the Parable of the Lost Coin; before the Parable of the Shrewd Manager

○ *Who is the author?*
Luke

○ *Who are the main characters?*
Jesus, father, two sons, and God

○ *Where in the biblical world did it happen?*
a parable, not an actual location

○ *Where is this in today's world?*
a parable, not an actual location

Find the full description of *Lay the Foundation* on page 15.

Did You Know?

✔ A parable is a simple story to explain an important lesson or point. Jesus used parables to explain many things including heaven and the Kingdom of God on earth.

✔ Luke is the only gospel writer to include the Parable of the Prodigal Son.

✔ The word *prodigal* means someone who is reckless and wasteful with money and other important resources. In this case, the son squandered his inheritance.

Pray

Dear God, we don't always make good choices. Sometimes we hurt the people who love us. Help us find our way back to the goodness and love of friends and family. Help us celebrate being welcomed back home. Amen.

Suggested prayer methods are outlined on page 15.

Share the Story

Suggestions for storytelling are detailed on page 16.

Respond to the Story

Invite each member of the group to use bricks and figures to respond to the story. This can be done individually or in small groups. Suggestions for how to support this form of theological reflection can be found on page 16.

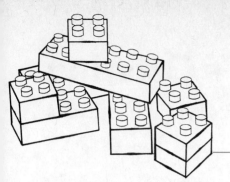

Building Questions

- ○ I wonder if you have ever been jealous of a family member?
- ○ I wonder if you have ever felt a parent has been unfair?
- ○ I wonder if you have ever made a choice you regret?
- ○ I wonder if a parent would ever refuse to help his/her child?
- ○ I wonder if you have a family member who has gone away?
- ○ I wonder if you have ever experienced forgiveness?
- ○ I wonder if you have ever offered forgiveness to someone else?
- ○ I wonder if it is ever hard to forgive?
- ○ I wonder where God might be in this story?
- ○ I wonder where you might be in this story?

Suggest Blueprints (if needed)

- ○ father
- ○ prodigal son
- ○ younger son
- ○ Jesus
- ○ God
- ○ welcome-home party

Share Responses to the Story

Encourage each group member to share the creations they have made in response to the story. More details about sharing can be found on page 17.

Share a Snack

- ○ party food: rolled meat and cheese, cut vegetables and dip

Note: A possible idea is for each member of the group to bring their favorite party food to share.

Continue the Story

One way to deepen the learning experience and create a link between group learning and faith formation in the home is to have builders show their creations to the adults who pick them up after class.

For additional study and conversation at home, consider different ways to share the Bible verses as well as some of the *Building Questions*. Possible methods of communication are texts, social media, e-blasts, website posts, or take-home sheets.

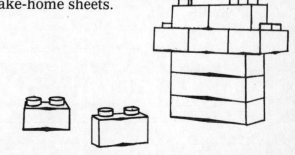

The Parable of the Prodigal Son

The Widow's Offering

Mark 12:41-44; Luke 21:1-4

Welcome the Group

Lay the Foundation

○ *Where is this story found in the Bible?*
New Testament

○ *What is its place in the Bible story?*
after Jesus answered questions about the resurrection; before the destruction of the temple was foretold

○ *Who are the authors?*
Mark and Luke

○ *Who are the main characters?*
Jesus, Sadducees, disciples, rich people, widow, and God

○ *Where in the biblical world did it happen?*
Jerusalem

○ *Where is this in today's world?*
Jerusalem

Find the full description of *Lay the Foundation* on page 15.

Did You Know?

✔ A widow is someone whose husband has died.

✔ The widow's offering is sometimes called a "mite", means a small amount.

Pray

Dear God, teach us that even little gifts and acts of love are important to you. Inspire us to be generous in all that we have and in all that we do (even if we don't think it is very much at all). Amen.

Suggested prayer methods are outlined on page 15.

Share the Story

Suggestions for storytelling are detailed on page 16.

Respond to the Story

Invite each member of the group to use bricks and figures to respond to the story. This can be done individually or in small groups. Suggestions for how to support this form of theological reflection can be found on page 16.

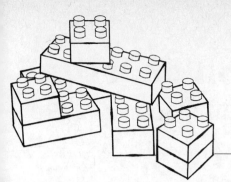

Ask Building Questions

- ○ I wonder what it would be like to have Jesus as a teacher?
- ○ I wonder what I can give to God?
- ○ I wonder what Jesus meant about the gifts given by rich and poor people?

Suggest Blueprints *(if needed)*

- ○ Jesus
- ○ disciples
- ○ Sadducees
- ○ rich people
- ○ widow
- ○ coins
- ○ ways for you to give to God
- ○ God

Share Responses to the Story

Encourage each group member to share the creations they have made in response to the story. More details about sharing can be found on page 17.

Share a Snack

- ○ gold-coin chocolates
- ○ silver-dollar pancakes

Continue the Story

One way to deepen the learning experience and create a link between group learning and faith formation in the home is to have builders show their creations to the adults who pick them up after class.

For additional study and conversation at home, consider different ways to share the Bible verses as well as some of the *Building Questions*. Possible methods of communication are texts, social media, e-blasts, website posts, or take-home sheets.

The Widow's Offering

The Temptation of Jesus
Matthew 4:1-11; Mark 1:12-13; Luke 4:1-13

Welcome the Group
Lay the Foundation

○ *Where is this story found in the Bible?*
New Testament

○ *What is its place in the Bible story?*
after the baptism of Jesus; before Jesus began his ministry in Galilee

○ *Who is the author?*
Matthew, Mark, and Luke each have their own account

○ *Who are the main characters?*
Jesus, Satan, angels and God

○ *Where in the biblical world did it happen?*
Judean Desert

○ *Where is this in today's world?*
West Bank, Israel

Find the full description of *Lay the Foundation* on page 15.

Did You Know?

✔ Jesus was out in the desert for 40 days.

✔ The number 40 is often associated with testing and the fulfillment of promises.

Pray

Dear God, sometimes we are tempted to do wrong things. Help us look to Jesus as the model of how to keep our eyes on you. Amen.

Suggested prayer methods are outlined on page 15.

Share the Story

Suggestions for storytelling are detailed on page 16.

Respond to the Story

Invite each member of the group to use bricks and figures to respond to the story. This can be done individually or in small groups. Suggestions for how to support this form of theological reflection can be found on page 16.

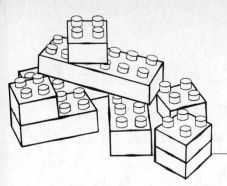

Ask Building Questions

○ I wonder if you have ever been to a desert?
○ I wonder when you feel tempted?
○ I wonder if you have gone for a long time without food?
○ I wonder if you know the difference between a *miracle* and *magic*?
○ I wonder if you have ever wanted more than what belongs to you?
○ I wonder if you have ever experienced something evil?
○ I wonder how Jesus felt when Satan was trying to tempt him?
○ I wonder how Satan was feeling when Jesus was refusing him?

Suggest Blueprints *(if needed)*

○ Satan
○ Jesus
○ God
○ desert
○ stone
○ Holy City and temple
○ kingdoms of the world
○ angels

Share Responses to the Story

Encourage each group member to share the creations they have made in response to the story. More details about sharing can be found on page 17.

Share a Snack

○ individual small loaves of bread
○ graham-cracker "sand" crumbles over ice cream or pudding

Continue the Story

One way to deepen the learning experience and create a link between group learning and faith formation in the home is to have builders show their creations to the adults who pick them up after class.

For additional study and conversation at home, consider different ways to share the Bible verses as well as some of the *Building Questions*. Possible methods of communication are texts, social media, e-blasts, website posts, or take-home sheets.

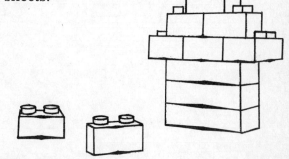

Jesus Enters Jerusalem

**Matthew 21:1-11; Mark 11:1-11;
Luke 19:28-40; John 12:12-19**

Welcome the Group

Lay the Foundation

○ *Where is this story found in the Bible?*
New Testament
○ *What is its place in the Bible story?*
**after Jesus healed two blind men; before
Jesus cleared the temple of money changers**
○ *Who is the author?*
Matthew, Mark, Luke, and John

○ *Who are the main characters?*
**Jesus, disciples, donkey, people of
Jerusalem, and God**
○ *Where in the biblical world did it happen?*
Jerusalem
○ *Where is this in today's world?*
Jerusalem

Find the full description of *Lay the Foundation* on page 15.

Did You Know?

✔ This part of scripture is often called "the triumphal entry."

✔ This is the reason we celebrate Palm Sunday.

✔ Jesus fulfilled the words of the prophet Zechariah (9:9) by riding in on a
donkey.

✔ Not everyone was glad to see Jesus.

✔ The word *hosanna* means "praise God."

Pray

*Hosanna, hosanna, hosanna! Praise God
now and forever. Amen.*

Suggested prayer methods are outlined on
page 15.

Share the Story

Suggestions for storytelling are detailed on
page 16.

Respond to the Story

Invite each member of the group to use
bricks and figures to respond to the story.
This can be done individually or in small
groups. Suggestions for how to support this
form of theological reflection can be found
on page 16.

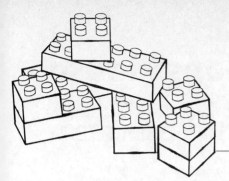

Ask Building Questions

- ❍ I wonder if it was ever hard for the disciples to trust Jesus?
- ❍ I wonder if it is hard for you to trust God?
- ❍ I wonder if you have been in a really large crowd?
- ❍ I wonder what it felt like to be in that Jerusalem crowd?
- ❍ I wonder if children were there?
- ❍ I wonder what words you would use to praise God?

Suggest Blueprints *(if needed)*

- ❍ Mount of Olives
- ❍ Jesus
- ❍ disciples
- ❍ donkey
- ❍ crowd
- ❍ parade
- ❍ palm branches
- ❍ clothing in the road
- ❍ God

Share Responses to the Story

Encourage each group member to share the creations they have made in response to the story. More details about sharing can be found on page 17.

Share a Snack

- ❍ party food
- ❍ parade food
- ❍ leaf/palm shaped cookies

Continue the Story

One way to deepen the learning experience and create a link between group learning and faith formation in the home is to have builders show their creations to the adults who pick them up after class.

For additional study and conversation at home, consider different ways to share the Bible verses as well as some of the *Building Questions*. Possible methods of communication are texts, social media, e-blasts, website posts, or take-home sheets.

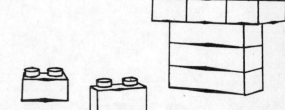

Jesus Cleans House

Matthew 21:12-17; Mark 11:15-19; Luke 19:45-48; John 2:13-17

Welcome the Group

Lay the Foundation

○ *Where is this story found in the Bible?*
New Testament

○ *What is its place in the Bible story?*
after triumphal entry into Jerusalem at the beginning of Holy Week; before Jesus cursed the fig tree

○ *Who is the author?*
Matthew, Mark, Luke, and John

○ *Who are the main characters?*
Jesus, chief priests, scribes, the people of Jerusalem and God

○ *Where in the biblical world did it happen?*
Jerusalem

○ *Where is this in today's world?*
Jerusalem

Find the full description of *Lay the Foundation* on page 15.

Did You Know?

✔ We often picture the moneychangers inside the actual temple, but some scholars believe the selling was taking place outside in the courtyard.

✔ It is also thought that Jesus was angry over the poor business practices (cheating) and not simply because things were being sold.

Pray

Dear God, thank you for making places for us to worship you. Show us how to use them in the best ways to glorify you. Amen.

Suggested prayer methods are outlined on page 15.

Share the Story

Suggestions for storytelling are detailed on page 16.

Respond to the Story

Invite each member of the group to use bricks and figures to respond to the story. This can be done individually or in small groups. Suggestions for how to support this form of theological reflection can be found on page 16.

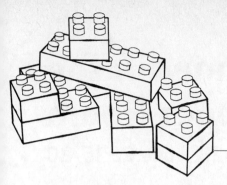

Ask Building Questions

○ I wonder what are okay things to do in a place of worship?
○ I wonder what things we should *not* do in a place of worship?
○ I wonder if you have ever felt cheated?
○ I wonder if you have been a cheater?
○ I wonder what was really happening in the temple?
○ I wonder why this is a part of the story of Jesus' death and resurrection?

Suggest Blueprints *(if needed)*

○ temple
○ temple grounds
○ marketplace
○ Jesus
○ moneychangers
○ chief priests and scribes
○ God

Share Responses to the Story

Encourage each group member to share the creations they have made in response to the story. More details about sharing can be found on page 17.

Share a Snack

○ street food
○ hummus and pita bread
○ gold-coin chocolates
○ silver dollar pancakes

Continue the Story

One way to deepen the learning experience and create a link between group learning and faith formation in the home is to have builders show their creations to the adults who pick them up after class.

For additional study and conversation at home, consider different ways to share the Bible verses as well as some of the *Building Questions*. Possible methods of communication are texts, social media, e-blasts, website posts, or take-home sheets.

A Dinner in the Upper Room

Matthew 26:26-29; Mark 14:22-25; Luke 22:15-20

Welcome the Group

Lay the Foundation

○ *Where is this story found in the Bible?*
New Testament

○ *What is its place in the Bible story?*
after Judas betrayed Jesus; before Jesus prayed in the Garden of Gethsemane

○ *Who is the author?*
Matthew, Mark, and Luke

○ *Who are the main characters?*
Jesus, disciples, and God

○ *Where in the biblical world did it happen?*
Jerusalem

○ *Where is this in today's world?*
Jerusalem

Find the full description of *Lay the Foundation* on page 15.

Did You Know?

✔ The term *Passover* comes from God "passing over" the Israelite homes with marked doorposts as told in the Book of Exodus. The blood on the doorposts was a sign to keep them safe from the angel of death while they were still in Egypt.

✔ The Feast of Unleavened Bread is another name for Passover.

✔ Jesus was in Jerusalem to celebrate the Passover with his disciples.

Pray

Dear God, help us to remember you when we gather together. Let bread and wine be two of the many ways you show your love. Let us walk with you as your beloved children. Amen.

Suggested prayer methods are outlined on page 15.

Share the Story

Suggestions for storytelling are detailed on page 16.

Respond to the Story

Invite each member of the group to use bricks and figures to respond to the story. This can be done individually or in small groups. Suggestions for how to support this form of theological reflection can be found on page 16.

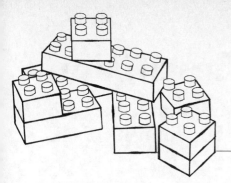

Ask Building Questions

○ I wonder who gathers together with you for special meals?

○ I wonder what your family does to remember the stories of God?

○ I wonder what your family does to remember special family stories from the past?

○ I wonder what food is served at your family gatherings?

○ I wonder if a friend has ever hurt you or done mean things to you?

○ I wonder what it would be like to have dinner with Jesus?

○ I wonder if any words for this story sound familiar?

○ I wonder if this story reminds you of something we do together in church?

○ I wonder what you think happens to the bread and wine when the priest blesses them?

Suggest Blueprints *(if needed)*

○ Jesus
○ disciples
○ upper room
○ Passover lamb
○ bread
○ wine
○ images of Holy Communion
○ God

Continue the Story

One way to deepen the learning experience and create a link between group learning and faith formation in the home is to have builders show their creations to the adults who pick them up after class.

For additional study and conversation at home, consider different ways to share the Bible verses as well as some of the *Building Questions*. Possible methods of communication are texts, social media, e-blasts, website posts, or take-home sheets.

Share Responses to the Story

Encourage each group member to share the creations they have made in response to the story. More details about sharing can be found on page 17.

Share a Snack

○ lamb or other meat

○ pita bread, matzo, tortillas, or other unleavened bread

○ traditional foods served for Passover: hard boiled eggs, herbs dipped in salt water, red grape juice, apple-nut paste (*charoset*), lettuce, and horseradish

○ bread and wine from common plate and cup

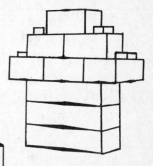

The Crucifixion

Matthew 27:32-66; Mark 15:21-47;
Luke 23:26-56; John 19:16-42

Welcome the Group

Lay the Foundation

○ *Where is this story found in the Bible?*
New Testament
○ *What is its place in the Bible story?*
after Jesus was handed over by Pilate to be crucified; before Jesus' resurrection
○ *Who is the author?*
Matthew, Mark, Luke, and John

○ *Who are the main characters?*
Jesus, Mary, John, Pilate, two thieves, Simon, Mary Magdalene, centurion, Joseph of Arimathea, Salome, Nicodemus, and God
○ *Where in the biblical world did it happen?*
Golgotha
○ *Where is this in today's world?*
Jerusalem

Find the full description of *Lay the Foundation* on page 15.

Did You Know?

✔ Crucifixion means to be killed by being bound or nailed to a cross.

✔ The crucifixion is the portion of Jesus' story most often told on Good Friday.

✔ The meaning of the word *Golgotha* means "place of the skull" in Aramaic and Greek.

✔ The Church of the Holy Sepulchre is located on the site believed to be the place where Jesus was crucified. The church, built in 330 AD, is located within the old walls of Jerusalem and still stands to this day.

✔ The word *passion* when used in the phrase "passion of Christ" describes the suffering of Jesus during this death on the cross. The root of the word *passion* comes for the Greek word meaning "suffer."

✔ Casting lots was a way of randomly making a decision or choosing a winner. The process is similar to rolling dice, playing rock-paper-scissors, or drawing the "short" stick. People often used bones or rocks to cast lots.

Pray

Dear God, your love for us knows no end. We thank you for the life of Jesus. He has shown us how to live and, through his death, we will live with you forever. Help us to remember the stories of Jesus and share them with the world. Let us never forget the amazing gift of your love and forgiveness. May we continue to live in your hope and joy all of our days. Amen.

Suggested prayer methods are outlined on page 15.

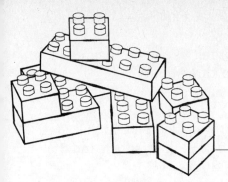

Share the Story

Note: As adults, we have become accustomed to hearing the story of the death of Jesus, but for some children, this will be the first time they hear the full story of Jesus' crucifixion. Telling the truth is important, as is facing the horror. Be present to listen to and process this story with the children, who *are* capable of understanding its facets—from the terror of the suffering to the love shown by God through Jesus. Take your time on this lesson, and avoid the temptation to hurry past the pain and run headfirst into Easter joy. We all need to know and feel the Good Friday part of our common story.

If you are not pairing the crucifixion and resurrection stories, please be sure to end the story sharing with a few words about Jesus' resurrection. Good Friday is important but thankfully not the end of the story.

Suggestions for storytelling are detailed on page 16.

Respond to the Story

Invite each member of the group to use bricks and figures to respond to the story. This can be done individually or in small groups. Suggestions for how to support this form of theological reflection can be found on page 16.

Ask Building Questions

- ○ I wonder who thought up the idea of crucifying people?
- ○ I wonder why some people wanted Jesus to die?
- ○ I wonder if the people were sorry after Jesus was dead?
- ○ I wonder what it was like to help Jesus carry the cross?
- ○ I wonder what sign *you* would make to describe Jesus?
- ○ I wonder what the two thieves thought when Jesus wouldn't save them and himself?
- ○ I wonder why Jesus didn't save himself from dying?

- ○ I wonder what it felt like to be covered in the darkness for three hours?
- ○ I wonder if you have ever sat in darkness?
- ○ I wonder what it was like to be in the temple when the curtain was torn and the ground was shaking?
- ○ I wonder if you have ever called out to God?
- ○ I wonder why the priests and other leaders were so afraid of Jesus?
- ○ I wonder if leaders thought they made a wrong decision?
- ○ I wonder if you have ever made a wrong decision?
- ○ I wonder if you ever had a chance to change your mind?
- ○ I wonder what it was like for John and Mary to become a new kind of family?
- ○ I wonder what would have happened if God saved Jesus from the cross?
- ○ I wonder what would have happened if Jesus had run away?
- ○ I wonder what it felt like to watch Jesus die?
- ○ I wonder what God was feeling when Jesus died?
- ○ I wonder what it was like to place Jesus' body in the tomb?
- ○ I wonder how hard it was to roll the stone over the opening?
- ○ I wonder what Jesus' friends and followers thought was going to happen next?
- ○ I would what it felt like to be without Jesus?
- ○ I wonder if you have ever felt like you were without Jesus?
- ○ I wonder what the word *messiah* means to you?
- ○ I wonder if you have heard this story before?
- ○ I wonder who was the first person to tell you about Jesus?
- ○ I wonder who you want to tell about Jesus?
- ○ I wonder what Jesus wants to tell you?

Suggest Blueprints (*if needed*)

- ○ Jesus
- ○ cross
- ○ Simon carrying the cross
- ○ the crowd
- ○ Golgotha
- ○ the thieves
- ○ Jesus on the cross
- ○ Mary and John at the foot of the cross
- ○ darkness
- ○ Jesus when he died
- ○ Joseph putting Jesus in the tomb
- ○ the tomb

Share Responses to the Story

Encourage each group member to share the creations they have made in response to the story. More details about sharing can be found on page 17.

Share a Snack

- ○ pretzel stick "crosses"
- ○ sips of vinegar (*gall*)
- ○ pita bread
- ○ grape juice
- ○ water
- ○ hot cross buns

Note: This may be another opportunity to "fast" from a snack during the lesson. Good Friday is one of the few days appointed for fasting throughout the church calendar year. Be sure to warn parents if you do not intend to provide snack, as usual.

Continue the Story

One way to deepen the learning experience and create a link between group learning and faith formation in the home is to have builders show their creations to the adults who pick them up after class.

For additional study and conversation at home, consider different ways to share the Bible verses as well as some of the *Building Questions*. Possible methods of communication are texts, social media, e-blasts, website posts, or take-home sheets.

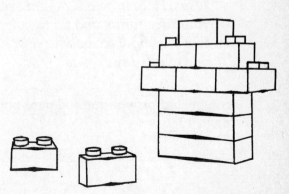

The Resurrection

Matthew 28:1-10; Mark 16:1-12; Luke 24:1-12; John 20:1-10

Welcome the Group

Lay the Foundation

○ *Where is this story found in the Bible?*
New Testament

○ *What is its place in the Bible story?*
after Jesus' crucifixion and burial; before Jesus appeared to Mary Magdalene

○ *Who is the author?*
Matthew, Mark, Luke, and John

○ *Who are the main characters?*
Jesus, Mary Magdalene, other female followers, some of the disciples, and God

○ *Where in the biblical world did it happen?*
Jerusalem

○ *Where is this in today's world?*
Jerusalem

Find the full description of *Lay the Foundation* on page 15.

Did You Know?

✔ The resurrection is the story of how Jesus returned to live after being dead in the tomb for three days.

✔ Each account by the gospel writers name different people as being present at the tomb. They also all describe the angel(s) who shared the news of Jesus' resurrection differently.

✔ John is the only gospel writer who does not mention an angel at the tomb.

✔ The resurrection is the part of the Jesus story we hear about on Easter Sunday.

✔ Islam considers Jesus a prophet.

✔ Jesus' tomb was actually similar to a small cave.

Pray

O God, who gives life to all living things, we thank you for the resurrection of Jesus. Help it be a sign and symbol of your love for us and the whole world. Show us how to look for new life each and every day. Amen.

Suggested prayer methods are outlined on page 15.

Share the Story

Suggestions for storytelling are detailed on page 16.

Respond to the Story

Invite each member of the group to use bricks and figures to respond to the story. This can be done individually or in small groups. Suggestions for how to support this form of theological reflection can be found on page 16.

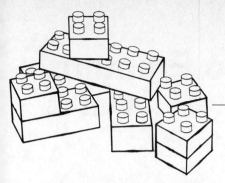

Ask Building Questions

○ I wonder what the friends and followers were doing during the three days Jesus was in the tomb?

○ I wonder what God was doing and thinking during the three days Jesus was in the tomb?

○ I wonder how it felt for Jesus' friends to see the empty tomb?

○ I wonder what angels really look like?

○ I wonder why angels always tell people, "Don't be afraid"?

○ I wonder if you have ever lost a friend?

○ I wonder if you have ever witnessed anything so surprising that you wanted to run away?

○ I wonder what it was like for the women to meet Jesus along the path?

○ I wonder if Jesus has ever come close to you?

○ I wonder what would have happened if Jesus stayed dead?

○ I wonder what it means to you that Jesus was raised from the dead?

○ I wonder what you might be wondering about in this story?

○ I wonder if you have heard this story before?

○ I wonder who was the first person to tell you about Jesus?

○ I wonder whom you want to tell about Jesus?

○ I wonder what Jesus wants to tell you?

Suggest Blueprints *(if needed)*

○ empty tomb

○ angels

○ Jesus alive

○ God

○ stone, rolled away

○ friends and followers of Jesus

Share Responses to the Story

Encourage each group member to share the creations they have made in response to the story. More details about sharing can be found on page 17.

Share a Snack

○ tomb buns (Wrap crescent rolls wrapped around a marshmallow; when baked, the center melts away to leave an empty, sweet space.)

○ hummus and pita pocket "empty tombs"

○ easter eggs

○ party food

Continue the Story

One way to deepen the learning experience and create a link between group learning and faith formation in the home is to have builders show their creations to the adults who pick them up after class.

For additional study and conversation at home, consider different ways to share the Bible verses as well as some of the *Building Questions*. Possible methods of communication are texts, social media, e-blasts, website posts, or take-home sheets.

The Road to Emmaus

Luke 24:13-35

Welcome the Group

Lay the Foundation

○ *Where is this story found in the Bible?*
New Testament
○ *What is its place in the Bible story?*
after Jesus appeared to the women at the tomb; before Jesus appeared to the 11 disciples
○ *Who is the author?*
Luke

○ *Who are the main characters?*
Jesus, Cleopas, another follower, and God
○ *Where in the biblical world did it happen?*
road to Emmaus
○ *Where is this in today's world?*
approximately 7 miles north of Jerusalem

Find the full description of *Lay the Foundation* on page 15.

Did You Know?

✔ This story is believed to have taken place on the evening after Jesus' resurrection.

✔ The word *Emmaus* means "warm springs" in Hebrew.

Pray

Dear God, you put the warmth of Jesus in our hearts. Let us celebrate that Jesus is always with us, even when we don't realize it. Amen.

Suggested prayer methods are outlined on page 15.

Share the Story

Suggestions for storytelling are detailed on page 16.

Respond to the Story

Invite each member of the group to use bricks and figures to respond to the story. This can be done individually or in small groups. Suggestions for how to support this form of theological reflection can be found on page 16.

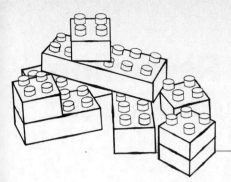

Ask Building Questions

○ I wonder if you have ever lost a friend?

○ I wonder if you have taken a long walk with a friend?

○ I wonder if you have ever felt like the last person to know something important?

○ I wonder what the disciples felt like after the death of Jesus?

○ I wonder if you have ever felt warm and happy when you were near someone?

○ I wonder why you felt that way?

○ I wonder if you ever felt Jesus close to you?

○ I wonder if you ever remember Jesus when bread is broken?

○ I wonder what it feels like to see someone you miss?

Suggest Blueprints *(if needed)*

○ Jesus

○ Simon

○ unnamed follower

○ the road to Emmaus

○ God

○ bread and wine

Share Responses to the Story

Encourage each group member to share the creations they have made in response to the story. More details about sharing can be found on page 17.

Share a Snack

○ pita bread and hummus

○ matzo

○ grape juice

○ long "road" fruit leathers

Continue the Story

One way to deepen the learning experience and create a link between group learning and faith formation in the home is to have builders show their creations to the adults who pick them up after class.

For additional study and conversation at home, consider different ways to share the Bible verses as well as some of the *Building Questions*. Possible methods of communication are texts, social media, e-blasts, website posts, or take-home sheets.

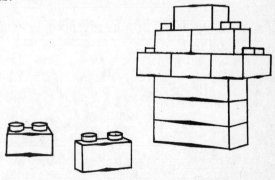

The Ascension
Mark 16:19; Luke 24:50-53; Acts 1:1-11

Welcome the Group

Lay the Foundation

○ *Where is this story found in the Bible?*
New Testament

○ *What is its place in the Bible story?*
after Jesus appeared to the disciples; before Matthias was chosen to replace Judas as a disciple

○ *Who is the author?*
Mark and Luke

○ *Who are the main characters?*
Jesus, disciples, and God

○ *Where in the biblical world did it happen?*
Bethany

○ *Where is this in today's world?*
West Bank city of al-Lizariya

Find the full description of *Lay the Foundation* on page 15.

Did You Know?

✔ Saint Luke wrote both the Gospel of Luke and the Acts of the Apostles.

✔ The ascension was Jesus' return to heaven 40 days after his death and resurrection.

✔ To "ascend" means to "go up."

✔ The mountain where Jesus was standing was called Mount Olivet (Mount of Olives).

Pray

God, we thank you for sending Jesus to be with us on earth. We also give you thanks for promising to never leave us. Even though Jesus returned to heaven, help us to remember that Jesus' love surrounds us each day. Amen.

Suggested prayer methods are outlined on page 15.

Share the Story

Suggestions for storytelling are detailed on page 16.

Respond to the Story

Invite each member of the group to use bricks and figures to respond to the story. This can be done individually or in small groups. Suggestions for how to support this form of theological reflection can be found on page 16.

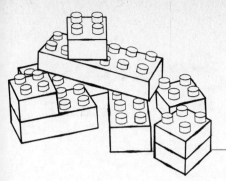

Ask Building Questions

- ○ I wonder if something has ever happened where you couldn't believe what you were seeing?
- ○ I wonder if you have ever been blessed?
- ○ I wonder if you have ever blessed anyone?
- ○ I wonder what a blessing from Jesus might sound like?
- ○ I wonder why Jesus couldn't stay on earth forever?
- ○ I wonder how the disciples felt when Jesus returned to heaven?
- ○ I wonder when Jesus might return?
- ○ I wonder what the power of the Holy Spirit feels like?
- ○ I wonder what stories the disciples told about Jesus after he went back to heaven?
- ○ I wonder what stories you will tell about Jesus?

Suggest Blueprints *(if needed)*

- ○ heaven
- ○ Jesus
- ○ disciples
- ○ Bethany
- ○ Jesus ascending
- ○ clouds

Share Responses to the Story

Encourage each group member to share the creations they have made in response to the story. More details about sharing can be found on page 17.

Share a Snack

- ○ cotton candy or marshmallow "clouds"
- ○ olives
- ○ pita bread and hummus
- ○ vegetables and fruit
- ○ cut fruit with yogurt "clouds"

Continue the Story

One way to deepen the learning experience and create a link between group learning and faith formation in the home is to have builders show their creations to the adults who pick them up after class.

For additional study and conversation at home, consider different ways to share the Bible verses as well as some of the *Building Questions*. Possible methods of communication are texts, social media, e-blasts, website posts, or take-home sheets.

Pentecost
Acts 2

Welcome the Group

Lay the Foundation

○ *Where is this story found in the Bible?*
New Testament

○ *What is its place in the Bible story?*
after Matthias was chosen to replace Judas; before Peter healed a crippled man

○ *Who is the author?*
Luke

○ *Who are the main characters?*
Disciples, Holy Spirit, and God

○ *Where in the biblical world did it happen?*
Jerusalem

○ *Where is this in today's world?*
Jerusalem

Find the full description of *Lay the Foundation* on page 15.

Did You Know?

✔ The root word for "Pentecost" means "fiftieth" in both Greek and Latin.

✔ In Old Testament times, Pentecost was the Jewish Festival of Weeks, a celebration of the harvest and the celebration of Moses receiving the Ten Commandments.

✔ In New Testament times, Pentecost is the observance of when the gift of the Holy Spirit was given to the disciples.

✔ Pentecost is often called "birthday of the church."

Pray

Holy Spirit of God, come into our hearts with love and light. Help us to burn with your love and shine in the world. Amen.

Suggested prayer methods are outlined on page 15.

Share the Story

Suggestions for storytelling are detailed on page 16.

Respond to the Story

Invite each member of the group to use bricks and figures to respond to the story. This can be done individually or in small groups. Suggestions for how to support this form of theological reflection can be found on page 16.

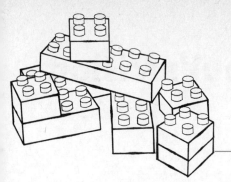

Ask Building Questions

- ○ I wonder what it feels like to be filled with the Holy Spirit?
- ○ I wonder what a "tongue of fire" looks like?
- ○ I wonder how you would feel if the Holy Spirit rested on you?
- ○ I wonder how the Holy Spirit came into a closed room?
- ○ I wonder if you have ever been in a place that felt confusing?
- ○ I wonder what you know about the Holy Spirit?
- ○ I wonder what dreams you dream?
- ○ I wonder if it was hard to remember Jesus after he returned to heaven?
- ○ I wonder who was the first person to tell you about Jesus?
- ○ I wonder if you know someone who doesn't know about Jesus?
- ○ I wonder if you know anything about the day you were baptized?
- ○ I wonder what it means to commit your life to God?
- ○ I wonder in what ways you praise God?

Suggest Blueprints *(if needed)*

- ○ closed room
- ○ Disciples
- ○ Peter
- ○ dreams and visions
- ○ Holy Spirit as wind
- ○ Holy Spirit as tongues of fire
- ○ Jesus
- ○ King David
- ○ baptism
- ○ God

Share Responses to the Story

Encourage each group member to share the creations they have made in response to the story. More details about sharing can be found on page 17.

Share a Snack

- ○ red-gelatin "flames"
- ○ watermelon
- ○ bread and grape juice
- ○ pita bread
- ○ red fruit leather
- ○ fondue

Continue the Story

One way to deepen the learning experience and create a link between group learning and faith formation in the home is to have builders show their creations to the adults who pick them up after class.

For additional study and conversation at home, consider different ways to share the Bible verses as well as some of the *Building Questions*. Possible methods of communication are texts, social media, e-blasts, website posts, or take-home sheets.

Saul's Vision
Acts 9:1-22

Welcome the Group

Lay the Foundation

○ *Where is this story found in the Bible?*
New Testament

○ *What is its place in the Bible story?*
after Philip and the Ethiopian eunuch; before Saul preached in Damascus

○ *Who is the author?*
Luke

○ *Who are the main characters?*
Saul, Ananias, Jesus, and God

○ *Where in the biblical world did it happen?*
Damascus

○ *Where is this in today's world?*
Damascus, Syria

Find the full description of *Lay the Foundation* on page 15.

Did You Know?

✔ Paul is also known as Saul of Tarsus.

✔ Saint Paul is considered the author of half of the New Testament books. These writings are in the form of letters to early church believers.

✔ Paul was not one of Jesus' disciples. He became a believer after Jesus returned to heaven.

✔ The name *The Way* was given to the early followers of Jesus.

✔ Paul tells of his conversion in three places (Acts 9:1-22; 22:1-22; 26:9-24.)

Pray

Dear God, you have called us all to love you and honor you. Show us how to be surprised by your wonderful ways and be ready to change our minds when needed. Help us be people who spread your love in the world. Amen.

Suggested prayer methods are outlined on page 15.

Share the Story

Suggestions for storytelling are detailed on page 16.

Respond to the Story

Invite group members to use bricks and figures to respond to the story, either individually or in small groups. Suggestions for how to support this form of theological reflection can be found on page 16.

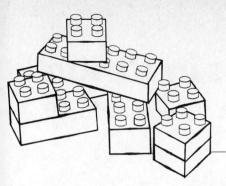

Ask Building Questions

- ○ I wonder if anyone has ever tried to hurt you?
- ○ I wonder if anyone has tried to tell you untrue things about God?
- ○ I wonder if you have ever met someone who is afraid of God?
- ○ I wonder if you have ever felt close to God?
- ○ I wonder if God has ever spoken to you?
- ○ I wonder what it is like to be healed by God?
- ○ I wonder if you have ever felt like you needed healing?
- ○ I wonder what it would be like to be blind?
- ○ I wonder how you could follow Jesus?
- ○ I wonder how you could use your life to help others know more about Jesus?

Suggest Blueprints *(if needed)*

- ○ Saul
- ○ road
- ○ bright light
- ○ people traveling with Saul
- ○ Jesus
- ○ Ananias
- ○ God

Share Responses to the Story

Encourage each group member to share the creations they have made in response to the story. More details about sharing can be found on page 17.

Share a Snack

- ○ popcorn "stones" from the road
- ○ pita bread and hummus
- ○ grape "eyes"
- ○ vegetables

Continue the Story

One way to deepen the learning experience and create a link between group learning and faith formation in the home is to have builders show their creations to the adults who pick them up after class.

For additional study and conversation at home, consider different ways to share the Bible verses as well as some of the *Building Questions*. Possible methods of communication are texts, social media, e-blasts, website posts, or take-home sheets.

Paul and Silas in Prison
Acts 16:16-60

Welcome the Group

Lay the Foundation

○ *Where is this story found in the Bible?*
New Testament

○ *What is its place in the Bible story?*
after the conversion of Lydia; before troubles with the church in Thessalonica

○ *Who is the author?*
Luke

○ *Who are the main characters?*
Paul, SIlas, family of a demon possessed girl, jailer and his family, God

○ *Where in the biblical world did it happen?*
Macedonia

○ *Where is this in today's world?*
Northern and central Greece

Find the full description of *Lay the Foundation* on page 15.

Did You Know?

✔ Paul was also known as Saul of Tarsus.

✔ Saint Paul is considered the author of half of the New Testament books. These are in the form of letters to early church believers.

✔ Paul was not one of Jesus' disciples. He became a believer after Jesus returned to heaven.

Pray

Dear God, help us to trust in you, even in scary times. Help us to remember your love and protection. Amen.

Suggested prayer methods are outlined on page 15.

Share the Story

Suggestions for storytelling are detailed on page 16.

Respond to the Story

Invite group members to use bricks and figures to respond to the story, either individually or in small groups. Suggestions for how to support this form of theological reflection can be found on page 16.

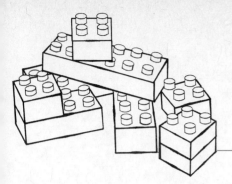

Ask Building Questions

- ○ I wonder if you have ever known someone who was blamed for something they didn't do?
- ○ I wonder if you have ever known someone in prison?
- ○ I wonder how Paul and Silas felt in jail?
- ○ I wonder if you have ever felt an earthquake?
- ○ I wonder if you have ever helped someone know more about Jesus?
- ○ I wonder if you have ever watched a baptism?
- ○ I wonder what it means to be a part of the family of God?
- ○ I wonder if Paul ever thought teaching about Jesus was too hard?
- ○ I wonder what helped Paul and his friends be brave?

Suggest Blueprints *(if needed)*

- ○ Paul
- ○ Silas
- ○ jailer
- ○ demon-possessed girl
- ○ jail
- ○ crowd
- ○ baptism
- ○ God

Share Responses to the Story

Encourage each group member to share the creations they have made in response to the story. More details about sharing can be found on page 17.

Share a Snack

- ○ pretzel-stick "prison bars"
- ○ graham crackers *(Build graham cracker "jails," then knock them down before eating them.)*
- ○ stacked up "walls" of applesauce or pudding cups
- ○ rice-treat square "prison walls"

Continue the Story

One way to deepen the learning experience and create a link between group learning and faith formation in the home is to have builders show their creations to the adults who pick them up after class.

For additional study and conversation at home, consider different ways to share the Bible verses as well as some of the *Building Questions*. Possible methods of communication are texts, social media, e-blasts, website posts, or take-home sheets.